HAYDN

AND

OTHER POEMS.

BY

THE AUTHOR OF "LIFE BELOW."

NEW YORK:
PUBLISHED BY HURD AND HOUGHTON.
Cambridge: Riverside Press
1870.

RIVERSIDE, CAMBRIDGE:
PRINTED BY H. O. HOUGHTON AND COMPANY.

CONTENTS.

A

DEDICATION TO A FRIEND,

AND AN

INTRODUCTION TO THE PUBLIC.

WHILE writing "Life Below," I was accustomed to place in your hands copies of the several books after their completion, in part for safe keeping, in part for the purpose of soliciting your friendly criticism. When I took them from you, in order to have them published, nothing could have been more appropriate for me than to return them to you in a public dedication. But older and weightier obligations claimed my first regard.

Now that the time has come when I can acknowledge the firm and disinterested friendship which encouraged me through struggles of apprenticeship, in connection with the acknowledgment I desire to express, in public, those conceptions of poetic thought and form upon which I have often dwelt in private. Not that I esteem them needed in order to interpret, to appreciative minds, my poetry. I feel indebted much — and doubly so, because all happen to be strangers to myself — to writers who have ventured to express, in public periodicals, opinions of my works, as favorable, certainly, as could be reasonably expected. It is true that much injustice, also, has been done me, as I think, in many cases. What, for instance, is more aggravating and absurd than that a man, simply because he has exhibited the fidelity of the artist while delineating an experience imagined, should be taken to task not only for commending, but even for possessing, characteristics of which he fancies that he has expressed disapprobation rather, inasmuch as he has represented them in a fictitious character not only, but even thus under a process of chastisement and correction? However, if I be inclined to find fault with the critics, on the score of superficiality, I am deterred by the consideration that my own examination of each latest publication of a similar character is equally defective. If poetry be never fitly finished, as is true, until the author have submitted it to microscopic tests in order to detect and to obliterate the least suggestion of a flaw, it is not fitly criticized before the reader have applied his mind to it with tests of equal thoroughness. But such tests will not be applied to any book until, in some way, it can indicate that it is worthy of them. Such an indication, as it seems to me, is best presented in the fact, that those who chance to read it once, re-read it. Wherefore is a book re-read? I think, since it expresses truth.[1] In popular phrase, men term the truth eternal. In it they find the sources of perennial freshness. And the degree in which a work of art embodies it, appears to me to measure the degree in which it can awaken a perennial interest.

And in the sphere of language, poetry, much more than prose, seems fitted to awaken such an interest; a fact which furnishes the key to all my theories presented at this time. The one who spake the truth in forms which have been held most sacred, and received most universally, spake never, we are told, without a parable. But parables are in poetic form. They illustrate a principle of real life through picturing how it operates in fancied circumstances. They indicate the workings of a law in one department or development of nature, through instancing its operations in analogous departments or developments. And parables are not exceptional examples confirming the esteem to which the truth, presented after such a method, is entitled. While new discoveries of successive epochs render obsolete the theories of

[1] Poetry, the flowering of literature, has a form, and, so to speak, an aroma peculiar to itself which cause it to appeal especially to the æsthetic faculty. Nevertheless truth will be found to constitute the root even of these qualities See pages 6, 7.

philosophers, they have, if any influence, an opposite effect upon the entire range of fables, myths, and legends which furnish subjects to the poets. Analogies implied in such, with morals pointed out for men who lived two thousand years ago, may be applied with equal truth to men and manners of to-day.

And if we turn from whole productions to short statements, we discover here, too, that the world remembers best those in the forms of poetry, — the proverbs, precepts, and quotations indicating illustrations from analogy. In these sometimes both objects, in which there are similar operations, are expressed; as, for example, "Anger, like rain, breaks itself on what it falls upon." Sometimes one object only is expressed with clearness, "Gratitude is the memory of the heart." And sometimes neither is expressed; a law alone is stated, which suggests, at once, a vast variety of objects to which it may be applied, and in which operations are analogous, "With what measure ye mete, it shall be measured to you again."

Such facts as these suggest the question whether analogy and truth are necessarily connected. He who thinks upon the subject will discover that they are. The truth which is the object of investigation in philosophy and science is the truth of analogy. The philosopher desires to know no isolated facts as ends, but that he may determine through their agency the laws and methods operating underneath them;

and may show in what respects these methods are identical beneath diverse phenomena. The truth upon which any scientific system can be founded, is a law, an operation, with analogies in all the different departments and developments of nature.

And these analogies, in so far as they really exist, present the mind with truth, as I believe, as nearly absolute as anything with which a human being can become acquainted. If similar methods operate through all the universe; and if these methods be indicative at all of thought, they indicate the thought of the Intelligence creating and controlling all the universe. When similar methods are made manifest in different deeds of a human being, they are recognized as characteristic, as Miltonic or Napoleonic. Why may not the methods manifest amid the different phenomena of nature be considered characteristic not only of the universe, but of the One who formed it? To the man who gazes with discrimination on them, why may not the laws which operate in matter, although underneath forms limited and transient, represent, symbolically and yet accurately, the absolute traits of character and the eternal laws of life which are the objects of perpetual adoration to those high intelligences nearest to the Deity? I have, at present, in my desk a pile of manuscripts, in which I have endeavored to develop this idea with special applications to the different arts. If life and health be spared, at some time I may finish them. At present, I can but suggest the very wide domain of thought to which the subject introduces one.

Not only do these indications of analogy embody truth; they constitute the essential element of beauty also. As expressed through a medium of speech, the simplest ballad is possessed of beauty chiefly in so far as it portrays the experience of some members of the human family after a method so accordant with the course of nature that the reader feels that it would be the experience of all its members, under circumstances similar in temperament and time. Descriptive poetry has beauty chiefly in so far as it suggests the operations of the general laws of nature through the outlines of the special forms which it delineates. It rises to a high degree of beauty, it becomes sublime alone when, like the poetry of Wordsworth, for example, it suggests resemblances between the methods of the material universe and operations of the mind. Upon the contrary, no mere collection, no mere crowding of comparisons, can add real beauty to a composition if these do not indicate analogies existing in the nature of things. When similar operations are exhibited in objects one of which does not exist in nature, as, for instance, when the mind is likened to a machine, or sunbeams to the spokes of a wheel, such indications of resemblance, though they may be forcible, are not apt to suggest ideas of beauty, nor do they any oftener suggest ideas of truth. For highest realization, these both demand expressions of analogies made evident through forms of nature. Beauty must have the dignity attracting to divine proportions; truth the sanction of the laws of the Creator.

With aid of this thought, I detect the difference between an effort of imagination and of fancy. It is the difference between an utterance of principle and of conceit, of wisdom grounded on a wide experience, and of a whim with no foundation whatsoever. The illustrations of the former, spring from natural and actual resemblances; those of the latter, from fictitious, artificial ones; and in so far as they do this, can be expressive neither of the true nor of the beautiful.

This fact, moreover, that both truth and beauty in their highest forms are traceable to a similar source, enables one to harmonize an effort to express the true in poetry with an effort to portray the beautiful; for no one must forget that beauty only is the ultimate end of poetry, as of each other art. And yet, may it not be the ultimate end of art, precisely in the way that blessedness may be the ultimate end of virtue? The spiritual aim is reached through truth to orderings of the Creator; may not the material aim be reached through truth to operations of creation?

And from this point of view, as it appears to me,

one can appreciate, too, the true position of the artist. Nature furnishes results in forms. The artist separates and recombines these forms in order to produce entirely new results. These are artistic, in entire conception or in portions, in the degree in which they are analogous to nature (ἀνά λόγος; i. e. thereon a word; a word in addition, a different expression of the same thing otherwise expressed in nature). Their work it is, to bear the same reports of beauty and of power which are transmitted through the sunshine and the storm; to tell, ideally, the same old tales of love and hate, of joy and suffering, which make susceptive human nature laugh and sigh along the pathway of its actual experience. And often, too, true art can yield results which furnish man more clear conceptions of the true and beautiful than are presented by results in nature. Sometimes upon the faces or the lips of human friends, there dawn more radiant glances, or there waken sweeter accents. At such times, from the intenser concentration of the love in them, we seem to gain a nearer and a clearer apprehension of what constitutes divine love, than a vague unincarnated agency could furnish us. So sometimes through the lineaments or tones of art which man produces, from the greater prevalence therein of human elements, thought is conveyed with power and plainness which could not be possible to the mysterious moods and mingled voices of the forests and the seas.

If this be true of art, what shall one say of him to whom we are indebted for portrayals of such a character? The artist is the priest of nature, in his rank inferior only to the priest of revelation. It is he who lifts the veils which hang about God's earthly tabernacle. It is he who steps within the holy place, who bows before the light which shines from the Shekinah, and who comes back to the masses bearing them a message from the Truth which dwells behind the symbol. If a man be disciplined through learning of God's truth, and if the methods operating under forms of nature indicate the truth, then art, in so far as it can reveal these methods more distinctly, does it not reveal the laws of God, too, and thus discipline mankind? Consider only the effects of novel literature, a single, and, perhaps, not the chief branch of literary art. There was a time when virtuous people feared its influence. And, certainly, poor novels are the poorest trash that ever thwarted time of thought. Yet really artistic novels, not distorting life for morals right or wrong, have they not an effect upon the reader like to that, and salutary, too, as that, which is produced through wide experience of the world?

As differing from the other arts, poetry has for its object to express analogies through a medium of words, and these analogies can be expressed not only in the thoughts communicated, but also in the medium of communication. To this do I attribute the significance of *style* in poetry. For contrary to theories of some poets, all the world of readers have attributed to it a very high significance. It is true that here, as elsewhere, it requires a master's hand to rescue art from artificiality. But it is true, as well, that here, as elsewhere, if one lower his aim through fear of failure, the success which he proposes will be failure far more fearful. Words have truth and beauty and a history embodied in them. In its first conception, every utterance was given both a sound and sense, and, if compound, a structure fitted to resemble, in the sphere of form, experiences of consciousness, or of relations between different experiences of consciousness, existing in the sphere of thought. And these analogies expressed in epithets, are still perceptible in every language, and are recognized as an essential element in causing style to be poetic. Notice the analogies in the following passages, sometimes in single epithets, sometimes in combinations of them:—

> That all the *jarring notes* of life
>   Seem *blending* in a psalm,
> And all the *angles* of its strife
>   Slow *rounding* into calm. — *Whittier*.

> *Raging* appetites that are
> Most *disobedient* and *refractory*.

Your life, good Master,
Must *shuffle* for itself.

If I have a conscience, let it *sink* me.
This new and gorgeous *garment*, majesty,
Sits not so *easy* on me.

Nothing could have *subdued* nature
To such *lowness* but his unkind daughters.
Shakespeare.

Not, therefore, am I *short*
Of knowing what I ought.
One *sip* of this
Would *bathe* the *drooping* spirits in delight.
His easy steps *girded* with *snaky wiles.* — *Milton.*

To teach the *young* idea how to *shoot.* —*Thomson.*

The *toiling* pleasure *sickens* into pain. —*Goldsmith.*

The *spumy* waves *proclaim* the watery *war.*
Love *stood* the *siege*, and would not *yield* his breast.
Dryden.

It is needless to multiply examples. The fact that these analogies in single words are found in purest forms in languages while in their infancy, before long use or misuse have made trite or obsolete their first significance, is one cause why its earlier productions, as a rule, rank highest in the history of a nation's poetry; a rule, however, which applies much less to English than to other languages. For in our compound tongue well-nigh all technical and hackneyed terms, as well as words employed by unprecise, illiterate writers, are of Latin origin. The simpler Anglo-Saxon synonyms are left by them almost intact, to be employed, with their full force and freshness, by the writers of a higher order. What a difference in power and picturesqueness, for example, between Saxon words like *draw back*, *strip off*, and *up-right-ness*, and their synonyms of Latin origin, *retire*, *devest*, *integrity*.

If language in its earlier stages be poetic, we must draw the inference that poetry itself is something which must be ascribed to nature rather than to culture. This view is confirmed by noticing not only how all people in uncultivated nations, but how children of our own race live, as men say, in imagination; with what aptitude they recognize resemblances between things new to them and others more familiar. Their seniors, too, when under strong excitement, as of love or piety, and apparently when most oblivious of results of culture, grow unexpectedly poetic. Judging from instances like these, some have affirmed that poetry is different from prose, in that the former is the language of the feelings, while the latter is the language of the intellect. This certainly is not an accurate distinction. The tendency to poetry may be occasioned by the state of feeling, but is really caused by intellect itself endeavoring to give form to thought for which it has no form at its command. It is not at command of savage or of child, simply because no form appropriate has come, as yet, within their very limited range of information. It is not at command of the cultivated man, because, to his excited mood, all forms, though multitudinous, with which he is acquainted, seem inadequate. Accordingly the uncultured and the cultured are impelled alike to originate expressions for themselves. And these expressions, inasmuch as they present intangible sensations according to the analogy of tangible perceptions, are, like all terms in their incipiency, poetic. But they are really the results of intellect. Thought, in its very essence, is comparison. The poetic state, in which the tendency to use comparisons is in the intensest exercise, may be the state of mind in which there is the intensest exercise of thought. What though this thought may be occasioned more by an excited state of feeling than by calm deliberation? Is it therefore to be disesteemed? Are not the vast majority of words of sympathy and love occasioned thus? And have they, therefore, less of eloquence, of truth and beauty in them, than the more deliberate utterances of policy and sycophancy? Or, as a fact, have poets less of truth in what they furnish us than writers of mere prose? Are not the spirits of great poets, notwithstanding all their quickness of perception and expression, subject unto them? Milton and Dante, were their works inspired by frenzy? Shakespeare and Goethe, were they not well-nigh as great philosophers as poets? In these latter days, when all the world reflects, can any poet reach high rank who is not philosophical? I know that just now there is a reaction. We have had too much prolixity, and now, forsooth, we must have too much prattle! Do men think the baby cannot prove as stupid as the dotard? Would it not be better to maintain a medium ground? Between extremes, the one too plain for wit, the other too obscure for wisdom, is a sphere of thought in which philosophy and poetry may be united.

Two processes exist which men term philosophical. The one proves through analogy, the other through induction. The former is addressed to judgment mainly, and is recognized immediately. The latter is addressed to reasoning mainly, and is mediately recognized through steps of logic. Upon all occasions when its circumstances so affect the mind that its perceptive overbalance its reflective powers, — as is the case with all the members of a savage and uncultivated race, with children, and with older persons in the presence of exciting causes, — then the mind expresses thought according to the dictates of the judgment rather than of reasoning; of intuition, I might almost state it, rather than of understanding. Precisely these conditions are those which, as has been shown, give birth to poetry.

It follows, therefore, that philosophy, so far as it

can argue from analogy, may overlap the sphere of poetry. If, in addition, it express its proof in *language* of analogy, may it not be poetical in form as well as substance? There is one book, the Bible, which combines more poetry with more philosophy than any other composition in the world. And I am well-nigh certain that the poets of our own day, if they would produce results which after-years shall value for intrinsic truth and beauty, should recur, more frequently, like the great poets of antiquity, not only to religious themes, but also to the methods of expression in the books of revelation. Aside from sacredness which has preserved them for the pious, the influence which these books exert to-day, and have exerted through so many generations, over irreligious minds, is proof that there is something in the forms embodying thought which they present, to make them models worthy of attention from all literary artists of all time.

To resume my line of thought, prose is not different from poetry as thought from frenzy, or philosophy from fantasy; but rather in the circumstance that, while the former is the language natural when reflection is predominant, the latter is the language natural when perception is predominant. The writings of the lesser or occasional poets are produced amid excitement which, at intervals, avails to paralyze reflection, and to stimulate perception. Those of the greater, or artistic poets, are results in part of temperament, which causes sensibility to operate as much from inherent energy as from accidental suscitation; and in part of culture which has power to train the judgment as it can the conscience, by enlarging, with the range of observation, the appearance of relations which exist between the things observed.

For, as elsewhere, it is necessary to remember here that there is nothing rendered perfect without practice. The vivid and precise imagination of the artist, differs from the fancy of the amateur, as the executions of the music-master from the exercises of his pupil. By nature, woman's judgments are more accurate than her reasonings, and man's reasonings more accurate than his judgments. Through cultivation, the judgments of the one become more reasonable, and the syllogisms of the other more judicious. Through neglect of culture and inert reliance on the gifts of nature, the woman's composition runs to froth, the man's to sediment. But truth is never sentimental, beauty never commonplace. The finest mental products have been wrought by those in whom were blended best the powers of both sexes, — a truth which, by the way, like every truth, admits of comic treatment, and is caricatured in our own day by certain men with long hair and loose gowns, and women *vice versa.*

However, it is needless here to instance any

further thoughts suggested by my ramblings in the field of poetry. I add alone, what all who have read thus far will surmise, that theories like these have influenced my writings. Many of my poems, in their first conception, sprang from hints suggested by analogies. And thus whatever value they may have, has been enhanced in that, like everything in nature which expresses truth, they convey a general significance as well as a specific one; express, in short, a law of life. The "Destiny-Maker," for example, has a moral which may be applied to love, and yet with equal aptitude to other different experiences. The same is true of "Choosing." "Loving" has a plan revealing in a sphere of mind those principles of action and reaction everywhere apparent in the sphere of matter. Once again, since in the province of both science and religion there exists a tendency to classify all time and space and life, in races and in individuals, by separations into periods or parts of sevens, a classification analogous was attempted in the seven books of "Life Below." In order to complete the idea of life, the effect which each successive stage in the development of character produces on the world without, was indicated in short passages between the several books. These, outward sounds of the ascending stages of the inner life, were named according to the notes ascending in the musical scale. Some critics have detected in this plan a source of marvelous merriment. It is not sure, however, that the poem ought to bear the blame of this. Are there not some to whom all scientific classifications whatsoever seem ridiculous?

That in developing these theories, which, in my own experience, have been the offshoots of my practice rather than the germs of it, I have done aught more than to express with greater plainness truth discovered long ago, I do not claim. The writings of all greatest poets show that they have felt the force of these same principles. If, in what has been here unfolded, I have added any thought to their conclusions, it is merely fruit of that which had its flower in Goethe and in Wordsworth.

And yet it must be that all literary principles, as well as principles in science and religion, grow. Each age discovers new facts, and investigating these brings to the surface laws which modify or change all views of nature and the supernatural. To these views must the poetry of each succeeding age accommodate itself. The Germans of the generation just gone by, stand foremost in the ranks of modern literary art, because the foremost to accommodate their modes of thought and methods of expression to those modern views of mind and matter which philosophy and science in their country have developed, not alone for Germany but for the world. And thought advances still; and poetry, if it would satisfy the wants of our own age, must modify its bearing to the requisition. Just as Christ assumed the form of our humanity, in order that He might become the Saviour of the race, so he who would become an agent, in his smaller sphere and for a shorter time, to lead the thoughts of men toward any higher region, be he prophet, priest, or poet, must assume the phase of life for which he labors.

While this is true, however, it must not be thought that, for the current, one can sacrifice the classical. The genuine artist is distinguished just as much by comprehensiveness as by susceptibility. He can as little disregard fixed standards of all ages as the fickle theories of his own. And therefore is it that his works acquire their permanence. While many things controlling taste in one's own period shall pass away, the pupil of what has remained from former times may grow the master of what shall remain in times to come.

It has been shown that poetry can lift a man as near to regions of pure truth as can be possible for any merely intellectual agency. And while one yields allegiance to the Bible and to Christ, he must believe that intellectual agency can have an influence thereto by no means slight. There is a slavery to materialistic interests of earth which, though it be not all that is included in the sphere of sin, is, certainly, a large proportion of it; there is bondage to the spirit of this world, from which the simple truth has power to set men free.

In our own age, especially in our own country, notwithstanding many works of purest purpose and most certain merit, there exists, as many think, an opening, and, therefore, a necessity for art, not better, it may be, but different; for art which can do something more than has been yet accomplished toward infusing ideality and spirituality into the present. Where all the masses read, and where, by consequence, all are subjected to their influence, our literary men should feel the grave responsibility which rests upon them to improve the tastes and judgments of the people, as well as to be popular. And, therefore, though I do not wish to seem obtuse or bigoted, I must confess a craving for a literature of higher tone than that which is most prevalent at present; for literature which can afford some elements of wit more manly than orthography which echoes of the nursery; and principles of wisdom more profound than whimsical sophomoric skepticism, caught, almost by rote, from schools of Germany. Our writers must attune their themes to deeper and to higher notes, — notes in accordance with the spirit of the age, and, at the same time, with the truth both of philosophy and of Christianity.

Demand is everywhere the lever of supply. The nature, no less than the soul that asks, receives. If I be right in thinking that there is a vacancy, I certainly am right in prophesying that it will be filled. And toward effecting such an end, if my productions have no other influence than that of stimulating to achievement of enduring merit, writers who are my contemporaries, I shall feel that I have neither studied art nor written poetry in vain.

At the same time, I am thoroughly aware that those who undertake that which I here suggest, will venture on a field where must await them, at the first, much more of opposition than applause. To speak to one of benefiting him is to suggest of his deficiency. The chief reward of such, yet a sufficient one, as I conceive, must be derived from those experiences of thought and love which every effort in the realm of thought and love is fitted to develop in the agent of it. Like other laborers in this world, our writers, too, must learn that the achievements of this life are measurable, less by power exerted on the world without, than by capacity unfolded in the consciousness within; that to the mind of faith, the life, the most successful, may be that which to the eye of sense is failure most complete; that to the earnest worker still remains the vigor and the strength acquired by practice, even though, in the opinion of the world, all energy have been expended in vain blowing at the wind or talking with the echo.

This I say, because I think that such convictions

only have the power to lift one really above servility to current thought although he serve it; that with such convictions only will a soul look high enough — I would not say for its reward, but high enough for its authority to be a fitting delegate of Him who only is the Sovereign of all Truth, and whose eternal verity alone, when uttered through the lips of mortals, has a sanction valid to command an acquiescence either general or continued.

HAYDN.

THIS poem was suggested by the tale entitled "A First Love," in the "Musical Sketches" of Elize Polko. Her authority for it is based upon the historical fact that Doretta (Anne is the name which I find in the biographies) Keller had a sister beloved by Haydn, and who entered a convent. My own authority for the additional connection indicated in the poem between the marriage of Haydn and the influence of the father and the priest, is derived from such passages as these, which may be found in every biography of the musician: "Forced to seek a lodging" (*i. e.* when a boy, in Vienna), "by chance he met with a wig-maker, named Keller, who had often noticed and been delighted with the beauty of his voice at the Cathedral, and now offered him an asylum. This Haydn most gladly accepted: and Keller received him as a son. . . . . His residence here had, however, a fatal influence on his after life. . . . . Keller had two daughters; his wife and himself soon began to think of uniting the young musician to one of them; and even ventured to name the subject to Haydn. . . . . He did not forget his promise to his old friend Keller, of marrying his daughter Anne. But he soon found that she was a prude, who had, in addition, ... a mania for priests and nuns. . . . . He was himself incessantly annoyed and interrupted in his studies by their clamorous conversation. . . . . At length he separated from his wife, whom, however, he always, in pecuniary concerns, treated with perfect honor." — *Biographical Dictionary of Musicians.* 2 vols. London: 1827.

Such facts as these, taken in connection with the well-known piety of Haydn, are a sufficient warrant, as I think, for my imagined inference concerning the cause of his hatred of this "mania" in his wife. In the poem I have endeavored to bring the personality of the musician more vividly before the mind of the reader by use of the name Haydn, than would be done if I had caused the characters to employ his baptismal name, Joseph.

HAYDN.

HARK, sister! hear I not the vesper song?
And is it not my Haydn's melody?
Can we not lift the window? Is God robb'd,
Think you, if, while these forms of praise do pass,
Some breath of their sweet panting pause with us?

There — they have died away. — Why say men died?
Live they not still? — Sister, my body here,
Because it pulses, moves, and speaks out thought
And wakens thought in others, thus you know
That it has life. And music, while it sounds,
Does it not pulse and move and speak out thought
And waken thought in others? Yes, what though
It leave earth quickly? To those patient eyes
Which scan eternity, Time cannot be
The measure of true vital force. No, no,
Then heavenly lightning were a weaker thing
Than earthly smoke. The music fades away;
And do not bodies? Are their lives not like?
Only the music, it hath never sinn'd:

It hath not known a wish save that of God:
It need not linger long here. Dear, I dream,
In those grand halls of heaven, if there shall rise
Sweet echoes of our earthly lives, re-lived
Yet not as on the earth, that there shall rise
Echoes of earthly music just as real;—
At least of Haydn's. It has life breathed in;
Invests his soul. His phantom shapes of sound
Do make me thrill, as though a power did come
And clasp, with hands below these fleshy robes,
And touch, for once, as spirits do, the heart.
They woo me as a god might, who own'd heaven.

Why must I not talk thus? Better bid flowers
Keep back their perfume, dear, than bid our souls
Sweet with the bloom of love keep back sweet
    words.
I love him.—Shrink not, sister. You must hear.—
And say not I am weak. Should I not grow
Far weaker did I hold in such strong love?

We two lived long together, in one home;
He, both my brother and my lover too,
My helper, and my hero. All my youth,
It glow'd like sunrise round that warm, bright face.
My senior by four years was he; and yet

So delicate in his blunt, boyish way,
So young in all things save in being kind,
He did seem near to me. Before I knew,
E'en in the bud of girlhood, he had pluck'd
My blushing love. He wore it on his heart.
Yes, all my life did take root in his soul.

Now I remember once when we did stroll
Down through that vale whose furrow unannounced
Renders a mountain of the flat church-yard.
It was that time of year when nature seems
In mood most motherly, her very breath
Held in a mild suspense above a world
Of just born babyhood, when tiny leaves,
Like infant hands, do stretch to drain lush dews
From palpitating winds, and when small brooks
Do babble much, birds chirp, lambs bleat, and then
When, while all round is one sweet nursery,
It is not strange if men ape childhood too,
And lisp. — Ah me, minutest syllables
Are too coarse, still, for love's ethereal sense!

As was her wont, at that time walk'd with us
My elfish younger sister, Doretta,
My pride and Haydn's pet, her merry tones
Ringing, when we did wax too pensive there,

Like bells that lure too wind-wild bees toward
home,
And bringing flighty fancies back to earth.

But Haydn liked this not, would ward it off,
Turning her chafing overcharge of nerve
From tongue to foot, with "Here, Doretta, imp!
You cannot climb this ledge," or "leap that brook,"
Or "find those flowers"; — then bending down toward me,
"I do abhor our German prudery.
We two should walk alone, or else have four,
Or six. When two agree they make a match.
A third is but a wedge with which to split
The two apart."

And once he paused with me,
And while Doretta linger'd, hid from view,
We two sat languidly upon the turf.
"Spring!" he began, "I feel slight wish to spring!
Yet, maybe, our whole lives are like our limbs;
They must draw back, recoil, before they spring.
Our frames relax'd, they may make ready thus
To vault the new tests of the fresher year. —
What think you? — aye? — and is this not a law?
Must we not always crouch before we rise?

Must we not kneel before we know of heaven?
And, tell me, if one had some aim in view,
Some aim sublime, to make him proud, so proud,
Say, would he not do thus?"—

"Ha!" cried a voice,
And quick, Doretta's curls shook like a shade
Between his face and mine. She smooth'd his
brow;
And with a wreath of heart's-ease crown'd it then.
"There, there, my sweet heart, be at ease," she said.

"Do you take my head for my heart?" he ask'd.

"Nay," she replied, "I would crown both conjoin'd,
Your music and your muse; your head the means,
The motive power, your heart."

"What would love gain,"
Quizz'd he, "with all one's heart devoted to
One's head?"

"Would it not gain immortal fame?"
She said.

"And do you think," ask'd he, "that this
Could set the heart at ease?" Then, musingly,—
"I sometimes think that no hearts, if at ease,
Have earnest in them of immortal fame.
High worth is earn'd through effort. Much ease
here
May weaken life, like sweetmeats served ere meats,
Surfeiting appetite before it act."

"But come," he added, starting suddenly,
"The sun has touch'd the earth. Look! even now
Its hot, red disk makes the chill river steam.
We must away." And with this all walk'd home:
Nor did he find chance after that to end
That which he would have said to me alone.

Yet sister, of late, ofttimes I have thought
That those dear lips were making ready then,
When came Doretta, to breathe that to me
Which might have roused a resurrection here,
As righteously as blasts from Gabriel's trump,
Have open'd for me here a life of love.

Nay, do not bid me cease. I must talk thus.
It is not discontentment with my lot.

My heart, it suffocates. This feeling here,
It stifles me. I think that one might die,
Forbidden speech. Sister, had you a babe,
A little puny thing that needed air,
And nursing too; and now and then a kiss,
A mother's kiss to quiet it; and arms,
Warm arms to wrap, and rock it into sleep;
Would you deny it these? Ah, dear, there is
A far more tender babe that God calls love;
And when He sends it, why, we mortals here,—
I will not say we grudge the kiss, the clasp,—
We grudge the little heaven-ling even air.
These tears, they will not stay: I weep to think
Of this poor gentle babe, this heir of heaven,
Smother'd because men are ashamed of it.
It is not strange that earth knows little joy
While men so little dare to speak of love.
For once (I ask no more) you will permit
That I should nurse this stranger, give it air,
Aye, aye, and food, if need be; let it grow.
It is God's child. I have no fear of it.

Haydn, he did not find chance after that
To speak with me; and this, I know not why.
My sire (e'en thinking this I know not why
My sire should aught surmise: we were alone,
Doretta, Haydn, and myself), my sire

From this time seem'd distrustful ; not that he
Loved less his favorite, Haydn ; but we both
Were still so young. And he, poor man, who earn'd
With all his toil but little, had a plan —
A dream, big bright beads strung on a flimsy
thread,
Mere lint brush'd from a worldling's flattery, —
That I should wed for wealth. So, like a gem,
I was lock'd up, for future use, in school.

There the strange faces drave my lonely thoughts
Back into memory for companionship :
And the dull books — and each one like a hearse
Wherein twice buried facts had been laid out —
Forced me to brood with self. I found my heart,
Bereaved of earth, lodged in an earth bewitch'd.

If Haydn present had call'd forth my love,
Absent, and thence conjured (how could I help ?)
He call'd forth worship. You remember, dear,
That those grand heroes of old Egypt seem'd
Not gods till taken from the eyes of men.
And so my Haydn, that bright world of his,
These never had appear'd so glorious
As then, when shut from me. Each slightest hint
Of his home made it seem a very heaven.

Sister, I often think that the real heaven
Must be so very bright; because, you know,
That even here the past is bright; and there,
Up there, we shall have faith, such perfect faith
That we shall not fear for the future. No:
It shall seem just as joyous as the past:
And with all bright, behind us and before,
Where shall be place for gloom? Ah, even here
Could there be gloom if only man had faith?

Three years pass'd over me. Can I forget
That beauteous summer's day which set me free?
At first, as though I had no soul at all,
I seem'd a part alone of the wide air:
And then all things had souls. The very earth,
My fellow, it did breathe! I felt its heart
Throb in the trembling breeze. I saw, far off,
The grand hills heave and fall, like pulsing breasts;
Then, this great life broke up in many lives,
All one through sympathy. In lieu of clouds
The gusty breeze caught up the twittering lark·
And shook the laughter from his nervous sides
Till all that heard did shake, the littlest leaves
Buzzing on trees about, like bees that swarm.
Then reverence hush'd all sounds, while, greeting
me,
Our dear old spire did mount a sinking hill,

And our home reach around a slow-turn'd rock.—
Then all stood still with Haydn! My hot cheek
Felt soon Doretta kiss me; and my sire;
When with bewilderment, as from a dream,
At last I awoke.

And what a dawn was that!
As if the sun had drawn earth to itself,
I dwelt in central light: and heaven, high heaven?
It felt some rays, perhaps, just touch'd by them,
There, at the star-points, but no more, no more.

Doretta had developt much: so fair,
In the first flush of ripen'd maidenhood,
I did not wonder while I watch'd his eyes,
My Haydn's eyes, that he did crave the fruit.
And they were intimate. Right merrily
From morn to night I heard their voices chime.
But Haydn did not seem to know me now:
He was so quiet and reserved with me.
Alas, but my heart flutter'd like a bird's
At his approach: my strange will, it flew off;
And, as if poised in air and not in me,
Left my weak words and ways without control;
And I remain'd as though I prized him not.

At last his illness came. How pale he lay!
We fear'd for him, lest life might slip its net:
The fleshy cords seem'd worn to such thin gauze!
But how his soul did shine through them! Its
light,
I will not say that it did gladden me.
Yet (is it strange?) while sitting by his side,
Fanning toward him fresh air which his faint lungs
Were all too weak to draw there for themselves,
For that so gentle, babelike sufferer,
I lost all fear. True to my womanhood,
I loved him more for his low, helpless sighs
Than ever I had loved him for his strength.

Often I thank'd my God that I had power
To think, speak, do for him what he could not.
I knelt: I gave my body to his soul:
I would yield brain, lips, hands, all things to him.
And was I not paid back? Ah, his sweet heart!
Each slightest beat of it, I felt it thrill
Through my twice dear, since doubly-serving veins.
And this was love! You know what Christ hath
said:—
That they alone who lose it find their life.
'Tis true. No: none can feel this consciousness
Of real existence till he really love,
And yield his life to serve some other's life.

"To serve Christ's," you say? Nay; one part of love,
By Christ's humanity, is serving man.
I speak a law of life, a truth of God:
I dare as little limit it to heaven
As to the earth: whatever be his sphere,
One knows not life therein until he love.

True love has life eternal, infinite.
Complete in its own nature, craving naught,
It needs no future and no boundary
Outside itself. Its own reward, I deem
It waits not on return. For 'tis more bless'd
To love than to be loved, to be a God
Than be a man.

At least, my love bless'd me
More than it could bless Haydn. I could try.
Yet, after all, Doretta was the one
Who only could succeed in aiding him.
She had dwelt long at home, learn'd household arts,
While I had but a bungling hand for them.
And so it happen'd that my task became
To fan him while he slept. When he awoke,
Though his meek lips would move with no complaint,

Nor fixt eyes glance for other than myself,
I could not do for him as sister could.
She would adjust his pillow, tell him tales,
Bring flowers, books, pictures, just what pleas'd
him most.
But to my heart that patient face, those eyes
Seem'd like such holy things! My deeds were
hush'd:
I did not dare disturb the silence there.
I do not think that it was selfishness;
Yet I was all content to look at him.

And my inaptitude my sister knew.
And partly since she knew what I did not,
And partly since she loved as well as I,
Soon as she heard his waken'd voice, she came
And sat by him until he fell asleep.
And then, when there was little to be done,
Then only was I left alone with him.

Sometimes I lean'd above his couch, and grieved
To think that I could do no more than this;
Sometimes I sigh'd, in thankfulness, that God
Would let me do so much. Once, praying thus,
Mayhap, He granted answer; for I thought
That, even though I might not have her art,

Doretta's art, at least that I might have
As much, perhaps, as guardian angels have;
For, without hands or voices, they keep watch
In spirit only. Still, when sister came,
I thought once more, that, if those souls unseen
Can envy, sometimes they may envy men.

Hard did I strive against this jealousy:
I plead with Mary, and I knelt to Christ:
I sought the priestly father and confess'd
My sinfulness to him. He chid me not
One half so much as I did chide myself.
How he did shame me that I dared to love
"A man who had not ask'd me for my love!
A man who loved my sister and not me!"—
He bade me count my beads from night to morn;
And one whole week I slept not, counting them;
But while I kept thought fixt thus on my sin
It seem'd that my sin grew.

Dear, I have learn'd
That all existence looms to greet the soul
Much like a mirror, wherein unto him
That hath is given more of what he hath:
Smile at the world, and it gives back a smile;
Frown, and it gives back frowns; look lovingly,

And all looks loving; think sin, all seems sin.—
My soul! dream not that thy most secret fault
Can hide itself. Thy sin shall find thee out.
Before, behind, on each side of thee flash
Thy moods reflected. Do but tell the tale,
Nay, do but whisper, glance, or breathe one hint
Of what thou findest in the world, and lo!
In this, thy tale of it, earth reads thine own.

I wander much. There came a change at last.
Haydn was better; and one afternoon,
Suddenly, ere I knew that he awoke,
Upon my cheeks arose a burning heat,
While, past my mist of tears exhaled, there dawn'd
The empyrean of his open eyes.

"Johanna," murmur'd he, "Johanna, dear,
What?—Do you weep for me? I shall not die.—
Nay, do not rise, nor call Doretta yet.
Hist;—do not let her hear us. Why, my friend,
Can you not stay with me when I awake?
What has Doretta told you?

"'Cannot do'?—
You think you 'cannot do for me'?—do what?
Have I ask'd you, dear, to do anything?

I pray you, stay here; do not anything.—
What pretty cuffs!—There, there: let it lie still,
That little hand: I like to look at it.—
Who said that I wish'd flowers, books, prints, and
tales,
And bustlings all about?—Who told you this?—
Your sister?—She has been a good, kind nurse:
And have you, too, not been a good, kind nurse?
Think you that I have never lain awake
In the long nights while you have watch'd with
me?—

"You have 'done but your duty'?—Say not so.
My friend most pleases when, forgetting due,
She seems to do her pleasure: and my foe,—
Who does not shrink to feel one near enough
To freeze him with a chill though duteous touch?
Duty is but the body part of love:
Let love be present, and this body seems
The fitting vestment of a finer life:
Let love be absent, 'tis a hideous corpse!
Ah, dear, I crave the soul, I crave the life:
Then rattle not a skeleton at me.

"I 'mean your sister'? Why?—Did I name her?
Did I quote her as being duteous?—

'Who do I mean, then'?—Little fluttering bird!
Suppose you were some real little bird,
How could you tell whence came or whither went
The wind that ruff'd your feathers?—Do you
know,
You women always will match thoughts to things?
You chat as birds chirp, when their mates grow
bright;
You love when comes a look that smiles on you.
We men are more creative. We love love,
Our own ideal long before aught real:
Our halo of young fancy circles naught
Save empty sky far off.—And yet those rays
Fit like a crown, at last, about the face
Which fortune drives between our goal and us!

"Still, all miss truth at times; none more than
those
Most prone to deem themselves infallible;
None more than men, who, fallible in proof,
Yet flout the failings of a woman's guess.—
And your guess?—it went right. I thought of her,
Your sister. We both honor her, and much.
And yet I fear for you, lest her strong will
Should overweigh by aught your strength of will.
For God has given you your own moods, dear;
And are you not responsible for them?

And if you yield them up too readily,
Not meaningly, yet may you not mistake?
Our lives, remember, are not sounding-boards,
Not station'd, senseless all, behind vain tongues
That prate, made wise in naught by our resound.
If you but echo back some other's wish
Think you God's mission for yourself fulfill'd?
Yet, dear, I would not chide; I caution you.
Wit heeds a hint; 'tis folly questions it.

"And so you thought, did you, that I wish'd flowers,
Books, prints, and tales, and bustlings all about?
Does not this earth, then, weary one enough
That he should need that others weary him?
You must have thought that I lack'd exercise!
I have seen nervous mothers shake their babes.
I never deem'd it wise. I am quite sure
That friction frets the temper of the child.
It is not natural. God does not shake
The ground with earthquakes when He wishes spring.
Life is not driven but drawn from its germs
By still, bright heat. Johanna, look at me.
I am too weak now to be driven toward life.
Nay, nay, I must be drawn! Dear, look at me.
Ah, I could tell of orbs bright as two suns.—

Nay, do not blush, and turn that face away.
Do you dream, then, that I wish sunset, eh?
The colors are right pretty, but — there, there —

"What? — I? I dare not face you now! Those
eyes,
Are they too bright? or loving? Love, like God,
Is it so brightly dear, that our poor lives,
Our vapory lives, like dews before the dawn,
Dare not to face it lest we melt away? —
Then be it so. Johanna, look! I dare!
Am I not yours? Can you not use your own?
Ah, dearest, I wish no life, naught, save you!"

Then, while he spake with his hands clasping mine,
And his eyes tiring mine with so much sight
That the weak lids were vext to feeble tears,
Doretta came.

But at our startled looks
She only smiled; said, "Haydn, what! awake? —
And you, Johanna? — You have been too good
Not to call me before. How kind in you!
Why, after all, a little training thus
Might make you like, perhaps, to be a nurse, —

Or housekeeper. — Your room was dreadfully
Disorder'd, dear. Our sire just came from it.
He was so cross!"

And I remember'd then
How unexpectedly I had been call'd,
This morn, to watch with Haydn. And I thought
That she had not been kind to speak of it.
I could have told her so; but check'd the words
And went my way, sadly and silently,
In hope to satisfy, at least, my sire.

This done, I sought my room, and wept and pray'd,
Thinking if I should tell my sire of it,
Of Haydn's love; or if I should tell Haydn;
And if he loved me still, since sister's words.
If only he could know my soul in truth,
I felt that I could suffer anything;
Could die, if so the veils about my heart
Could be withdrawn and show him how I loved.
Alas, I did not know then, had not learn'd,
That love may bear tests worse than even death.

The sunset brought Doretta to my room;
And she began, and chided me, and said,

"How dared you talk with Haydn? What said
you?—
He lies so ill, the fever high, so high.
He did but rave. How could you lead him on?
He may grow worse. O, sister, he may die!
And all come of your nursing. Sister mine,
When will you learn to learn what you know not?"

With this she sigh'd again, "If he should die?"
And then she told me such a long, sad tale,
Of how much store she placed upon his life;
How they had sung, read, thought the self-same
things:
She knew the closest chamber in his soul,
And what key could unlock it. Then she named
This, that, another man among our friends,
Surely she could not love them so;—no, no.

Then cried she, "O, my sister, had you search'd
Through all the world, its lonely, barren wastes,
And found one little nook; and had you work'd
And till'd it well, and form'd a garden there;
And had you watch'd the plantlets grow until
All dainty bowers bent over you with shade,
All sweet with bright buds and with singing birds,
What would you think of one who came and stript

Your life of this last thing which you lov'd so?—
Dear, I say not if God, if any power,
Should wrest from me my Haydn, this sweet soil
Whence spring all hopes which shelter my lone
hours,
And make it a dear thing to see and hear,
What would you think of it? Yet, sister mine,
You have not known and tired of many men.
You have not search'd, as I have, through the
world"—

"Nay, sister," said I, "I have not."

Then she,—
"Right: and you cannot yet know love, true love.
You were kept close at school: and it was hard
And it is harder still that you must wait,
As I have done, at your age too. But yet
Right love is ripe love. Life must be exposed
To sun and storm, pressing and bruising too,
Its fruit grows mellow by-and-by alone."

"Why, dear," said I, "I think that I can love!
You know what Haydn sings:—'Maidens, like
flowers,
Are sweetest when pluck'd in the bud'?"

"There now,
You always will be quoting him!" she cried.
"He is a man, ah yes, your first man-friend!
And yet, unmatch'd by you with other men,
How know you him, what sort of man he is?—
Girls unsophisticated are like bees:
They buzz for all, and yet sip all their sweets
From the first flowery lips that open to them."

"Nay," answer'd I, "I like him not for that,
Because he is a man!"

"Ah, ha!" said she,
"So you have shrewder plans?—I know, I know
It would be well if you, or I, could feel
That it were fixt, about our wedded life;
So many ifs and ifs, it vexes one;
It would be well now were the business done.—
We have such trusting natures, we poor girls;
Weak parasites we are: each tall, stout man
Seems just the thing that we should cling about.
But, dear, I think that half these trunks may rot:—
The wonder is that we dare cling at all!"

"But, Haydn," ask'd I, "Haydn?"—

"As for him,"
She sigh'd, "well, he may not be trustless all;
Yet if he be or be not, how know you
Who know not human nature, nor have learn'd
To analyze it and detect the truth.
Nature grows grain and chaff. Sift out the first
And cultivate it: it may yield you fruit.
That is the way with friendship."

"But," said I,
"If you should change yourself who change your friend,
Or but change his relations to yourself,
Or mistake ill for good, and till his ill,
Or, some way, make a new, strange man of him?"—

"I should till," answer'd she, "what pleases me;
And with what pleases me preserve my love."

"Sister," rejoin'd I, "not for future gain,
Not for what he may be, for what he is
I love my friend. I would not wish him changed.
I would not dare to risk, for my weak whim,
The perfect poising of relations which
God gave for me to find so lovable.

Ah, did I chiefly prize the possible,
Or profitable, where were present joy!
Nay, nay, I love that which I find possess'd."

"How much, pray, can you find possess'd?" ask'd
she.

"Enough to love," said I.

"What is enough
For that?" she ask'd again.

I answer'd her, —
"Enough to make his presence seem a boon;
Enough to make his wish seem a behest;
Enough to feel an impulse seeking him,
And, finding him, a consciousness of all."

"'A consciousness of all,' is vague," she said.
"I ask for reasons and you rave at me.
This very vagueness while you answer me,
It proves how immature in love you are."

"Sister," replied I, "there is higher love, —
A love of God, a love all worshipful;
And, should you ask me to define that love,
I might give back an answer still more vague.
The finite only can be well defined."

"The finite!" mutter'd she; and then exclaim'd:
"O, you wish worship! Well, then, we will find
A shrine, an idol, aye, a golden one.
— Forgive the simile. — You know our choice.
Our father's heart is set on it; and then
The baron could fall down and worship you;
So father says. Two idols you could have, —
Your home a very temple; only, dear,
You should not be so backward. With your choice —
These men, they all present their best to you.
You get the diamonds as if you were noon:
And I, I get the coals. — Humph, if I touch,
They either burn or else they blacken me."

This said, she left me quickly. It was strange,
What strange abhorrence shrank my soul from her
While speaking thus; less from her selfishness
Than her insensibility. Our tastes —
Those dainty despots of desire, our tastes,

Are our worst tyrants: they brook no offense.
I well-nigh hated her. Yet feeling thus,
While picturing her character as coarse —
Have you not noticed at the arsenal,
At times, while gazing on grim helmets there,
All suddenly, upon the polish'd iron
A wondrous brightness? then, in its pure depth,
Your own face hideous render'd? So with me:
Amid harsh outlines of her character
Shone soon its brighter metal: and from thence
Leer'd back upon my gaze my hideous self! —
For was not I the mean, the selfish one?
Had I regarded her, my father's wish,
Or the great baron's? — My soul answer'd, — no:
None except Haydn's.

Then I ask'd myself,
Could it be true, that which my sister said, —
That those sweet words of Haydn did exude
From some growth mushroom'd by disease? I thought
How marvelously crowded with strange shapes
Loom the deep halls of fancy lighted up
By fires of fever; and how trustingly
All weakness leans on all beside itself.
And soon I blamed myself that I did dare
To lure his poor, weak, crazed confession on;

And soon flush'd, too; and broke in passionate sobs,
To think that sister dared to hint such things.
So three days did my woes alternate; then
I went to my confessor with my cares.

"Well, well, my child," he said, "what! love, again?
The rest of us poor mortals here, we fret
Because we have too little of it, you
Because you have too much. I know, one hears
Of love, full oft, as of some great, grand thing,
But you have found yours, child, an elephant,
Taxing your whole weak powers to furnish food,
Yet of no use except to tramp on you.—
Tell me, think you that it is God, or man
Who makes much love so troublesome to one?"

"Why man," I said, "of course."

"My child," ask'd he,
"Do you not think it might be wise to get
Some less of man in you, and more of God?—
How fares it with your prayers?"

"But," I rejoin'd,
"It does not seem my fault, this woe of mine."

"Well, let us know," he answered, "weigh the
    sides:
Three wills against one will; now, which should
    yield?"

"Nay," I exclaim'd, "against two—me and Haydn;
And then, the other three have not such love."

"There, there," he said, "is that a Christian mood,
A modest, humble mood?—'Have not such love!'
How do we test love, child? It seems to me
That love, like light, is tested by its rays.
The halo is Christ's crown of royalty.
Self-sacrifice marks heaven's heraldry.
In all true life the strong must serve the weak;
The mother yields her pleasure to the babe;
The man to her; and Christ, God, to us all.
Ah, child, if you were strong! had but such love!"

I sobb'd, "I am not sure whom I should serve!"

"Well, put it thus:—your own wish or your sire's?
How reads the decalogue?"

"But," answer'd I,
"It seems as though there were some higher power
That one ought to obey, some power like God."

"Yes, child," he said, "the Church, surely, the
Church :
Of course, of course."

"Who is the Church?" I ask'd.
And then he laugh'd : "Who? — What a question,
child! —
Why, read your prayer-book. Why, the Church, of
course,
Speaks through its ministers."

"And if you speak,"
Inquired I, trembling, "if you give advice,
Is that the last word then? must I obey?"

"Something, perhaps, like that. But, dear me,
child,
You must not think us bears! We growl some-
times
In sermons, eh? — But then, dear me, dear me,

We would not eat our flock up, little lamb!—
Come," added he, "come, now; enough of earth;
We must look to your prayers."

Soon after this,
One day, while troubled much, I stumbled on
My Haydn, half restored, outside his room.
By chance he sat alone; and, seeing me,—
"Why, dear, what accident is this?" he said:
"And tears, too, tears?—Tell me, what sullen storm
Has left such heavy drops? Did it not know
That these, so tender eaves, might droop? if droop,
What rare views they might shut out from the world?—
What can have happen'd?

"Why not speak with me?—
You seem the very winter of yourself.—
Say, what has chill'd you so?—Surely not I?—
Johanna, I do know, whate'er my mood,
Did you but open those dear, rosy lips,
That summer air would be exhaled around
Sweet to dispel, calm my most stormy wish,
Despite myself!—Why will you trust me not?"

And then I spake to him. I hinted first
That I was odd: he should not mind my moods.

"Odd," answer'd he, "I knew a family
Where all the children were so very odd,
Like fruit, harsh to the touch and sour to taste,
Not ripe nor mellow. They had too much spring
And not enough of summer in their home.—
I know that you are not so very odd
As not to love to be with whom you love.
And can I not hope, dear, that you love me?"

And at these words (how could I help myself?)
My heart-gates sprang wide open. He learn'd all,
All that the priest had told me of myself;
And how we should not speak together more.

How wild it made him! Never had I seen
One shaken so. His anger frighten'd me.
"This wretched priest," said he, "you ask'd of God:
He answer'd you about the Church, 'of course,'
And of the Church about the priests, 'of course,'
And of the priests about himself, 'of course.'
I tell you this is cursed selfishness;
I tell you it is downright sacrilege;

Straining the thunders of the Infinite
Down through that sieve, his windpipe, dribbling out,
'I deal the voice of God, I, I, the priest!'"

"O, Haydn," cried I, "Haydn, how dare you!"

"Dare?" said he, "dare? You must think me a
dog,
A dog or woman cringing to a man, —
The more he kicks, the more to lick his heels."

"Haydn," I answer'd, — and I sobb'd aloud,
"I kneel down to his office, not to him."

"Poor girl," said he, "forgive me — stop — I
beg —
What? — do you think that I would make you
weep?
It was not of you, darling, not of you,
But of the system that I meant to speak."

"The system," I repeated; "Haydn, dear, —
Dear Haydn, you are not a Christian, then."

"And wherefore not?" ask'd he.

"Because," said I,
"You reverence not the Church."

"It was not that,"
He answer'd, "but the priests; of them I spake."

"Yet," I rejoin'd, "the priests have been ordain'd.
Have you no reverence for God's ministers?"

"God's ministers!" he mutter'd. "Yes; if God's!
I reverence the princeship, not the prince
When he forsakes his throne, and strips himself,
And puddles in the gutter with his slaves."

"What do you mean?" I asked.

"I mean that priests
Are not ordain'd to meddle with all tools.
Princes dispense; they do not mine their gold.
And priests administer the truth reveal'd.

Think you that they can mine unfathom'd depths
Of God's infinity; and bring to light
Laws not reveal'd, and govern men through them?
This, your priest, tampering with our social life,
Speaks with no warrant human or divine:
Whate'er his object, since he serves your sire,
Or since he fancies that my life, my gifts,
Might worthier prove devoted to the Church,
Is he in this our final arbiter?—
Have I no judgment?—Are you not of age?
Johanna, heed me; let no power, I beg,
Avail to sunder us. God hears my words.
I fear some scheme which may make your crush'd
heart
(It will ache if you yield) a stirrup trod
To speed some mounting meanness on toward ill."

"'Twas I," I said, "who craved the priest's advice."

"He handled the occasion," answer'd he.
"I would not dare to mould another thus.
Nay, though I knew that I could model thence
The best shaped manhood of my mind's ideal.
Who knows?—My own ideal, my wisest aim,
May tempt astray: they may lead him astray.
If I, made but to answer for one soul,

Take on myself the governance of two,
I may be doubly damn'd. 'Tis sacrilege,
This self-will which would manage other wills,
As though men were the puppets of a show,
And not souls, restless and irresolute,
In that mysterious poise 'twixt right and wrong
From which a sigh may launch toward heaven or
 hell. —
Dare you submit to this impiety?"

"But," ask'd I, "ought not one to heed advice?"

"Advice?" he answer'd. "Is this, then, the ground
On which these base authority? — Nay, nay,
Base where they may, their ground is wilfullness
Invested years ago; stript not for age
Which awes revolt! Shall your will yield to
 theirs? —
God has not given to over-strength of will
The right to rule right. Wilfullness is sin.
If you obey its mandate, how know you
That you obey not sin?"

"They may have will,"
I said, "but you forget; they are wise, too."

"About what?" he rejoin'd. "In other men
Experience is the warrant of advice.
But in the priest—what knows he of real life?—
Nothing: and if he give you his advice
He gives you nothing or he gives you whims;—
A bachelor teaching mothers how to breed!
Or fathers how to guide their grown-up girls!
Trust me, their counsels unversed, fancied, false,
Repel toward infidelity the wise,
And of the fools tempted to follow them
Make hypocrites or hypochondriacs."

"Nay," I said firmly, "I must hear no more."

"Have they then really separated us?"
He ask'd.

"How?" question'd I. "What mean you now?"

"Are you," continued he, "my friend, or not?"

"What is a friend?" I ask'd.

"What else," said he,
"But, in this world, where all misjudge one so,
A soul to whom one dares to speak the truth?"

"Ah, Haydn," ask'd I, "must one speak all truth?"

"Why not?" said he; "is sin less sin when seal'd?—
Is not the penitent a sinner frank,
The hypocrite a sinner not so frank?"—

"But," I protested, "may not truth do harm?"

"How so?" ask'd he. "If one show naked sin,—
Who knows?—then it may shame men from the sin.
And could the naked good accomplish more?
Are Christians not told to confess their faults?
Why should they not? Has real wrong such sweet smiles,
Such siren tones, that men should lust for it?
The harm comes from the lie, the mask of sin."

"But," I rejoin'd, "the young? the prejudiced?"

"For their sake," he said, "wisdom may be wise
In what it screens from folly.—Yet you know
The crime of Socrates,—'corrupting youth'?
The tale is old: this lying world hates truth.
Heed not the world. Rather speak out and die.
Our God is great. I deem Him great enough
To save His truth without subverting ours.
The Truth is sovereign. It is not a sham,
Holding high rank because men, courteous men,
Considerate men, allow it seeming rank!—
Who lies to save the truth distrusts the truth,
And disobeys God, and dishonors self.
Who strives to save a soul thus, loses it,
Trusting in evil and the evil one,—
Salvation through the devil, not through Christ!"

Then while he lay there with his flushing cheeks
Himself defending thus, I, charm'd the while,
The door flew open, and behind it stood—
My father and the priest.

If they had said
But one harsh word, it had not been so sad.

But they were kind, too kind. Ah, sister dear,
Have you not felt it, how much pain it gives,
This pain from kindness? Love is like the sun:
It brightens life, but may blast at times.
And when winds blow though man may screen himself,
And when rains beat though he may shelter find,
And when frosts chill though he may clothing wear,
What medium can ward off sun-stroke? — Love,
Its first degree may bring fertility;
Its second barrenness. It lights; it blights.
The flames of heaven, flash'd far and spent, turn smoke
To glut the gloom of hell!

And their kind words
(We could have braced ourselves against harsh means)
Wrought like a sesame on each defense
That caution should have held. "We did not know
Our own minds, poor young pair," they said. "At least,
True love could wait: and meantime, who could aid
Better than those whose treasure lay in us?"

And then to me alone they spake of Haydn: —
"He had been passionate: — how knew I that

His passion might not turn against myself?
And he had sinn'd, so sorely, sorely sinn'd: —
How could one talk thus of the Church and priest?
And did my love to him suggest such words,
Or should my love hereafter sanction them,
Might not his sin prove mine? — If I should yield,
Let his unbridled tongue win me, might not
My act confirm his trust in will uncheck'd?
And will uncheck'd, why, like an uncheck'd steed,
Once yield it rein — allow it once free way,
One false association of ideas,
Ideas still associate with the false:
There is no bridling after that: no, no."

I said, "He loves much."

They, "Had I not learn'd
That loss of friends is gain for fortitude,
But loss of fortitude gain for a fall.
Better lose love than life. Our characters
Expand through lifetime as the trees expand.
Each passing season that encircles them
Leaves from its clasp a ring: the ring remains.
So our past deeds remain about ourselves:
And men can trace them less from stories told,
Than from the range which circumscribes our mood,
Excluding or including right or wrong."

And then they added: "Might it not be found
That loss of my love was the very means
Design'd by Providence to chasten him?"

To this I answer'd, that "This love, his love
Itself seem'd Providence, a holy thing."

They only frown'd, and said, "The prince of ill
Came oft robed like an angel of the light;—
Why not like love?—The only holy thing,
Proved to be such, was Christ. What had He
done,
When moved by love? What of His sacrifice?—
And if I really loved this Haydn so,
What might love prompt in me?"

And thus they talk'd,
Till my faith welcoming doubt succumb'd to it;
And all that love which had made me so proud,
Which I had deem'd of growth so sweet, so fair,
Stung like a very thistle to my soul.
Each breath of theirs blew at its ragged shreds,
And sow'd its pestering seedlets far and wide
O'er every pleasant prospect of my life.

Thence I cried out in prayer. How I did plead!
How long, how toilfully, how fruitlessly!
At last, wild with despair, I left my beads,
And, as if it could cool a feverish faith,
Pass'd out and sought the night air. There I saw
The moon. It always soothed me with strange spells,
The moon. But now, as though all things had join'd
To thwart my peace, at once I saw this moon
Caught up behind an angry horde of clouds,
Chased with the hot breath of a coming storm
That clang'd his thunder-bugle through the west.
After the rude gust struck the moon, she tipt,
Spilling a single flash. Where it did light,
Just in the path before me, gleam'd a knife!—
Held up above a white dress! At the sight
I scream'd aloud. It seem'd a ghost!

My scream
Awoke no echo save Doretta's voice:—
"Well, sister, were you frighten'd?"

And to this,
Partly because the shock had stunn'd me much,
Partly because I felt me much provoked,

But mainly since my mood was deaf to sport,
I answer'd nothing. Whereat, as I think,
Though then in its unnatural, nervous state,
My mind surmised more horrid inference,
She, stirr'd to still more mischievous caprice,
Went on to vex me more.

"What?—You fear me!
Have you done aught, have you, against me, then?
And if you have, why should you fear a knife?—
Think, now, this blade might draw a little blood;—
What would that signify?—the body pain'd.
Suppose that one should wield some subtler blade
And draw a few tears, watery tears, weak things;—
What would they signify?—a soul in pain.
And did you never do that, now?—draw tears?—
And is the soul not something worse to harm
Than is the body?—Fy! why fear a knife?
If I supposed that through a life-time long
My soul must bleed its dear strength out in tears,
Say, would it not be mercy to that soul
If I should check the longer, stronger woe
By shedding a few drops of weaker blood,
Now, once for all?"

"Oh, sister sister mine,"
I cried out, still more frighten'd, "what mean you?"

"This," answer'd she, "I mean that I would cut
My body's life in two parts sooner than
My soul's life."

"Sister," I could only gasp,
"Cease — do ; — put up that knife " —

"Why ?" she replied ; —
"For what ? — Your wish ? Do you so often yield
When I wish aught ? — Tell me, what would you
give ?"

"Give ? — Anything !" I answer'd.

"Be not rash,"
She said. "It is not your way : and, besides,
The light is dim. — How know you ? may not ears
Be near us that may overhear ? Beware ! —
But pshaw !" she added, "I will go my way,
And you go yours. — Who cares what either do ?"

"Sister," I cried again, "you must not go !
Put up that knife ! — and if you will, then I —
I will not marry Haydn !"

"You?" she laugh'd;
"And who thought, then, that you would marry him?
Ha! and if I had wish'd to spring your thoughts,
Could I have chosen, eh? a shrewder thrust?—
Ha! ha!—to murder me, or you, or him!
It floods all madness just to tap your moods!
But go in, simpleton. You may get wet,—
And trust me with the knife. It meant no harm
Except to this beheaded cabbage here."

And, shaking this at me, she flitted off,
While I walk'd vaguely back, to find my room
Still sadder than before. I could not think
That my surmise was just; yet could not think
That all her strange demean was meaningless;
And to this day thoughts pause and puzzle oft
Pondering that scene: then, in my mood confused,
It seem'd the last blow which unsettled all.

What is more direful than the direful night
Spent by a man in trouble?—fill'd with fears
That sleep may bring distressful nightmares now;
And now, that morn may come before he sleep;
Until, betwixt the two, distracted quite,
Awake he dreams, and dreaming seems awake,
And evermore does weep at what he dreams,

And then does weep that he should dream no
more. —
In my dark fancies all that night I lay,
A murderess, guilty of Doretta's death.

Alas! and after those most woeful hours,
Awaited still more woe when morning came. —
Haydn, his shatter'd frame so frail before,
Rent by that throe of passion yesterday,
Lay, once more, prostrate in the arms of death:
So thought we all; I, ere I heard the fact,
Felt its cold shadow creeping over me.
The shutters closed, the silence everywhere,
The very coffin of our lively home, —
I did not need to ask the cause of gloom.
I mark'd my sire's sad look, and voice suppress'd;
I mark'd the kind physician, and no smile;
I sought and saw my Haydn. His pale face
Stared like a ghost's upon my fear of guilt:
For I, perhaps, had made his last works sin:
And I, perhaps, had help'd to doom his soul.

I thought then of my father, of the priest,
What they had said of love, and of true love,
Such love as Christ had had. I ask'd myself
If there was aught which I could sacrifice?

Sister, do you recall that afternoon
When first we met? How long, how sad it seem'd!
So many kindly sisters spake with me,
And pray'd for me; and then, at twilight dim,
When scarcely any eye but God's could see,
We knelt before the altar: and I rose,
Thankful if like that candle on the shrine
Within my heart one light alone did burn;
Yes, though all earth beside might be as dark
As those chill, shadowy chapels of the aisle.

I felt another life while I walk'd home.
Such conflicts come but seldom, like spring storms;
And though they may uproot and wrack the soil,
They find it frost-bound, and they leave it green.—
Alas! if grain or chaff be grown, depends
Upon the germs which they have wrought upon.
And yet, whate'er may come, it seems to me
Earth's happiness is hope; and every change
Caters to hope; and thus, before it break,
Each newest bubble charms us.

And it may bring
To every soul some real blessedness,
This sunrise of a new experience;
For with it dawns afresh the consciousness

Of how far past these present steps of Time
Wait for us those eternal eyes of God;
And all true thoughts of God are means of grace.

When he grew better (for our prayers were heard,
All of them answer'd: Haydn did not die)
The kind physician urged that I should not
Be wholly kept from him. But this, my sire
At first opposed: and then I went to him.

"Father," I said, "you need not fear for me.
If He will give poor Haydn health once more,
Then, I have vow'd to God that I will take
No veil save that which weds me to the Church."

"My daughter," he exclaim'd, "my daughter take—
What is this that you say?—you take the veil!
In God's name, girl, explain yourself."

"I made
This vow," I said, "before the virgin's shrine."

"What strange, what thoughtless deed is this?"
he cried.

"You take an oath?—oath not to be recall'd!—
That you will shut away from me this face?
This form so nurtured, these long waiting years?
This harvest of tired hope?—Nay, but I err;—
Correct me;—rather say my senses lie,
My brain has softened;—call me second child;
Bid to a nursery;—anything but this!

"True?—Is it true?—I would not frighten you:
Poor girl, God knows that you will have enough
To shudder for.—Yet, it bewilders me:
How did you, you who have been wont to be
Confiding and considerate and calm,
How could you do a thing so wild, so rash,—
Nay, I will not say disobedient,—
Nor once consult me?—Tell me this, my girl:—
What false seduction could have tempted you?"

"Father," I sobb'd, "I marvel'd when you said
That I could do so, then when I told you
That I would rather be a nun than be
The baron's wife."

"Why, my poor girl," he sigh'd,
"Those words were but in jest, whift off like breath

Blown at a fly that comes to trouble one.
And can it be that they?—I do believe
(My words have cropp'd in cursedness before)
The very atoms of the air, like dust,
Are spawn'd with vermin-eggs! If one but speak,
But break the silence; if his breath but bear
One faintest puff from passionate heat within,
Lo, it breaks open some accursed shell!—
It hatches forth foul broods of venomous life
That are blown back with the first changing wind,
To haunt him who provok'd their devilish birth!
By day they pierce us here, in our soft eyes;
By night steal through unguarded gates of sense
And harm our souls in dreams!—My heart! and
you?—
How could you deem those jesting words of mine
The voice of such deform'd desire as this?"

"But father," I replied, "the priest, your friend,—
At least, I think—so thought."

"The priest!" he cried,
"Has he been meddling with your malady?—
My friend?—He is my friend no more."

"Nay, I,"
I said, "I urged his counsel; even then
He said but little."

"Little!" he rejoin'd;
"That little was too much! Nay, never more —
Yet hold" — And here he paused. — "He is a priest. —
Daughter, now that I think, it need not all
Be darkness; no. — The priest — I have a clew
To clear this labyrinth — The priest, he may,
Aye, he shall get an absolution. Aye,
An absolution; we shall get that, dear."

And then my father, in his sanguine way,
Recover'd somewhat. And he fondled me.
"I see now; you love Haydn, my poor girl.
Why, here you are a woman when I thought
That you were but my pet, my little child. —
But do not weep: no; for I honor you,
My little woman! — There, forgive me now;
Forgive my quick words. When it comes, my girl,
The absolution, then, then we shall see
Whether the father can be kind or not."
With this he kiss'd me. And what could I do? —
How could I tell him that his hopes were vain?
How could I think myself that they were vain?

From this time onward came no further check
Attending Haydn. To the world he said,
My father, that "his daughter had his sense;"
That he "could trust his girl to be discreet;"
And to Doretta in some way he spake,
So e'en her caution was, in part, appeased.

Then days and weeks and months pass'd quickly by
In which, when Haydn's prison'd love would start,
E'en while I heard the trembling of its bars,
I learn'd to check him, saying, gently, then,
"But not now, Haydn; nay, but we will wait."

And thus a habit grew that our two lives
Dwelt like two friends, made separate by war,
Who, from the hostile camps, wave now a hand,
And now a kerchief, but who never speak.
And yet I cannot say love never spake.—
We did not mean it; but I think that love,
Like life, speaks truest when unconsciously.
What man is conscious where he touches God!—
There were but little deeds; yet Infinite Power
Is great beyond all measurements of space;
Love knows no measurements. There were but hints;
And yet what words of love yield more than these?

They hit the sense of love, but hit no sense
Where there is no love to receive the hint.

Our souls learn'd this at last; I wis not how.
And like two kittens playing on the hearth
We told our secrets, and none knew of it;
Nay, not ourselves: and still — nay, not ourselves.

How swiftly sped the hours through those dear
nights
When, after his long labors, he came home!
He had such winning ways of meeting me;
Call'd me such pretty names to make me feel
Like a small thing, that he might seem my Lord;
Teased me to tears that he might comfort me;
Or roused my temper that he might seem mild;
Or told such tales that in my dreams I laugh'd
At wit reflecting, though distorting his;
Or better still, play'd for me, ah, such strains!
The very thought of them refresh'd like dawn
While through the long night I remain'd awake
Half-conscious of the call of early birds
And sparkling spray of light dash'd o'er the dews.
At last, one such night, while we sat alone,
Some new impatience seized him; and he spake.

"Johanna, dear, allow me but this once; —
And say not, nay, say not that we will wait:
Have I not waited long? Johanna, mine,
What is the substance of this mystery
Whose shadow rests between us? Tell it me.
I know your slightest whisper would have power
To bid the intrusion off."

"Not," answer'd I
(I felt that now, at last, I must explain), —
"Not if the shadow, separating, fell
From some cause which no mortal could remove."

"How can that be?" he cried. "It cannot be:
Of old your father did oppose our love:
Of late he has grown so to favor it."

"And do you know," I ask'd, "what wrought his change?"

"What, save his wiser judgment?" he rejoin'd.

"Are there not," ask'd I, "courses in this life
Where conscientiousness and love may cross?"

"There!" he exclaim'd, "the old, old plea again!—
Your weakness is your wickedness. Why, dear,
Does not all conscience spring from consciousness?
And when is one most conscious? When unwell:
Slow-crawling blood frets limbs which are inflamed:
A sound man is not conscious of its flow.
And thus its morbid train of foul ideas
Vexes the soul diseased. But when in health,
When true to God and self, why need it feel
This conscience which is but the check whereby
God curbs the thought which has no love in it?—
If I be right, conscience cannot cross love.
Love may have freedom.

"Howsoe'er that be,
Conscience, at best, is but one element
Of character. The right mete leavens it:
The wrong may disproportion all its parts,
Sent like poor beer to froth and sediment;
The froth flown in the faces of one's friends,
The rest sunk down in self, embittering
One's own experience."

"But," I rejoin'd,
And interrupted him,—"this conscience in
Religion"—

"In religion; there," said he,
"This too much conscience, overbalancing
All wiser judgment, has made havoc worse;
Made men crave heaven and fear hell, so much
That in the gap, betwixt the two, was left
No charity with which to do good here
While on the earth."

"I hope that mine," I said,
"My conscience prompts my soul to do good here.—
What would you say were I, some day, a nun?"

He laugh'd so harsh, I shudder'd at his voice—
"'Were you a nun?' Dear, if those blooming looks
Bear wormy fruit like that, I ne'er will trust
Sound health again!

"Johanna, I could vow
That a nun's conscience is a consciousness
Of some vague pain which, in a nature form'd
Of body and of soul, may be a pain
Of which no mortal eye can trace the source;
From indigestion, muscles, nerves diseased;
From thought that puzzles and hence troubles one

As likely as from sin;—moods cured as well
By sunshine, clean clothes, larders full, good cheer,
As by gloom, filth, and fasting and long prayers."

Thus he continued till I would not hear.
I told him how "irreverent, unjust"—

"I might be both of these," he said, "if I
Urged that these poor souls were themselves to
blame.
Did I say this? No: for in these, our lives
Betwixt our immaturity and full
Maturity; betwixt credulity,
Nursed by fond trust in what some guardian knows,
And faith, nursed by that which one knows himself,
There is a realm where will is train'd to act
Through doubt and danger; where the character,
First wean'd from oversight, is taught to choose.
Then, like a tottling child, it yearns to cling
To some power greater which can act for it.
Its mood determines that to which it clings.
Some girls are giddy:—they are swift seduced.
And some are gloomy:—their beau is a priest.
Each plies the same work,—an accursed work,
That takes advantage of this weaker state,
And captures them for vice or veils, or both."

"But marriage is a capture, too," I said.

"Marriage," he answer'd, "is a natural state,
Made statelier through authority of law,
Which otherwise, might authorize mere lust.
A state to which, as not to convent life,
All social instincts prompt; may prompt still more
The more one's years. Who can forswear it
then?—
How can a maid, with half her moods unform'd,
At twenty, know the much changed temper which
May turn or torture her at thirty-five?—

"But— What, Johanna?—what now? You turn
pale!—
Were you in earnest?—Have you really thought?—
In God's name, darling, this can never be!—
Think only— Why should you?"

"Because," I said,
"I should hope to do good."

"And do you deem,"
He ask'd, "that the dear Virgin did no good,

While nursing her sweet babe? Was she no saint?
And what of Christ, who ate and drank with all,
Call'd glutton and a wine-bibber for it,
Was He no saint? Think, dear, what do men
need?—
To learn of life which never can be theirs?—
Nay, but to learn of life, of thought and love,
Which can make better all, of every class.
If you would be a saint then, O seek not
The way so different from the common path,
The truth so sunder'd from the common thought,
The love which knows no common sympathies."

"Are not some call'd," I urged, "especially
To take charge of the aged, sick, and poor?"

"Are not some call'd," he ask'd, "especially
To take charge of the men, too, whom they love?
Deem you it healthful for a soul still young
To yield up all affinity to age?
Is that truth, truth to nature, or to God?—
And may not vows, too hastily assumed,
Mask the true mission meant by Providence?—
Only when those of wide experience
Turn calmly from the world to convent life
Would I restrain them not. Let such find homes,
Large, sunny, healthful halls; and dwell therein.

Let them deal thence those gentle charities
So potent when dealt from a woman's hand.
It were not strange if sickness tended thus,
Lured by their gentle, loving smiles, should blush
Into all perfect health! if wickedness,
Beneath incrusted woes of worldly years,
Feeling the earlier faith of childhood waked
By woman's voice, should thus be born again! —
Renew'd for pure life in the soul as well
As in the body! All good has its place:
And I would not restrict this sphere for woman,
But rid it of its circumscribing vows."

"Of all vows?" ask'd I.

"Why not?" he rejoin'd.
"Do they not augment wrong, and, with it, woe? —
Once, I remember, that I spied a tree,
And vow'd that, through one hour, my eyes should not
Light on that tree again. What came of it? —
That vow kept me in misery through that hour.
And had it been a man and not a tree,
My vow had caused more misery, had it not?
And yet God has not made it wrong to view
A tree or man: — the vow, it makes the wrong.

"And, I remember, once I aided one,
A foe, that I might thus fulfill a task
Forced on me by my tutor. Prompted by
Free choice, my deed had been benevolence;
But the enforcement made it slavish toil.
And had a convent this same task enjoin'd,
Might its enjoinment not have displaced love?
Pure virtue is the child of liberty.
Better maintain this liberty of Christ."

"But Haydn," said I, "this strange convent, fill'd
With age and vowless maids — you banish thence
Christ-like self-sacrifice."

"Christ," he rejoin'd,
"Would not have died except to glorify
Himself as much as man, both equally.
The nun, does she thus glorify her race?
Or, feigning burial to human cares,
Humiliate rather her humanity? —
I must believe that souls not sever'd from
The world, but in the world yet not of it,
And in the body acting bodily,
The lives transfiguring our common lives
And common cares, these most resemble Christ. —

Poor prudes, to hint that truest womanhood
Is maidenhood! By Eve and Mary, no!
The mother is the model of her sex
And not the maid. False virtue and false vice,
To lift their own and lower the matron's rank,
Such ends they gain:—and is this sacrifice?"

"But they serve God," I said, "and others men."

"They do not serve God," answer'd he, with force.
"Talk not about that term, self-sacrifice.
Their deed is more akin to suicide.
God made our nature: he who yields it up
Yields up his manhood: this is suicide.
God made the world ruled by His providence,
Potent to train life: who leaves it leaves God:
This adds damnation unto suicide."

"But if he leave the world," I said, "that he
May enter thus the Church, he leaves not God.
Is not God in the Church?"

"What is the Church?"
Ask'd he.

"The kingdom of the Lord," I said.

"There," he exclaim'd, "look you, this Testament!
In it I read from Him, head of the Church,
That this same kingdom of God is within.
If so, have I no right to heed myself?—
My innate instincts, should I yield them up,
A passive slave to laws outside of me?"

"O Haydn," begg'd I, "say not this. It is
The same rebellion that I used to feel.
We should not judge for self, but reverence
The words of men who are ordain'd to teach,
The words of men who are so learned, too,
The words of councils fill'd with just such men.
Have you no reverence for authority?"

"Quite common charity would teach me that,"
He said. "And how could common piety,
If awed before the great eternal God,
Fail of a kindred reverence for all power?
The Church has power; yes, and I reverence it,—
Truth's storehouse, and historic guardian.
But are there no truths which have not been stored?

Infinity is broad. I would believe
The God within me and the God without;
In self, as well as in the Church and world.
And I believe that all that He has done
Has been done with a marvelous harmony.
And, when I love a soul as I love you,
Did all the priests on earth assemble here,
In front of them the pope, in front of him
A shining form put forth by them as Christ,
And tell me that this pure love lied to me,
I would not" —

"Haydn," I exclaim'd, "stop! stop!
You use such dreadful language. How dare you?—
And I have pray'd to God so much, so much,
That you might be submissive."

"I submit
To God," he said; "but with my love to God,
I cannot yield the godliest thing in me."

And there he sat, so firm and yet so mild,
I could not help myself, but I cried out, —
"Haydn, do not talk thus. You make me doubt."

"Would God," he said, "that I could make you
doubt:
Then might you learn true faith. Is there of will
One wise effect which does not follow doubt?
Is there one choice save from alternatives?
Doubt comes with wavering of the balances
Before the weightier motive settles down.
Let those who are so sure in church, in heart,
Solve me my doubt: — I dare to doubt of them
Whether they walk by knowledge or by faith.
I read that Jesus answers him who prays,
'Lord, I believe, help thou mine unbelief;'
That one hour ere His last success, He cried,
'My God, O why hast thou forsaken me?'
And so I deem that our doubts may not doom:
Rather they may be minor preludes here,
Ere our triumphant cadence, 'It is finish'd.'

"But, dear Johanna," added he, with warmth,
"Say to me, say, that you will yield them up,
These dreadful thoughts. Why, it would make of me
A very infidel! The Church destroy
Our love! Ah, then, what could it not destroy?"

Is it a wonder, that to such a mood
I could not say that which I would?

Months sped.
My time drew nigh. My vows must be fulfill'd.
I told my father of it, and he wept.
Poor man, he spent his hours alternately.
Sometimes he urged; sometimes he chided me;
Sometimes he kiss'd my cheek and look'd at me;
Sometimes he took me by the hand, and said,
"My daughter, dear, we must defer this thing;"
Sometimes he moan'd, "My daughter must do right."

Quite slowly dawn'd on Haydn's mind the truth,
Though not, as yet, the reason of my vow.
And all the household grew so mild with me;
And all the neighbors gazed so piteously:
Had my pale body lain within a shroud,
And had I loiter'd over it, a ghost,
Life had not seem'd so lonely and so chill.

One night I found my father still more sad
Than was his wont. I knelt before him then,
And "O, my father, why is this?" I ask'd.
But he said nothing. Then I question'd him:
I found the cause out. Haydn was the cause.
My father loved him so, more than a son;
And had hoped that he might be one indeed.

But they had talk'd together, and had talk'd
About Doretta. (Dear, forgive these tears)
My father sigh'd, and said, "All, all my plans
For all of you are vain!

"And why is this?"
Continued he, — "why this, that in my age,
When too old to renew aught, all are lost, —
My aims, my home, my hope, my happiness?
This is too hard for me, this punishment.
And for whom is it? Who has done such wrong
As to deserve it? — Here am I, myself.
I loved you, loved you both, look'd for your good
The priest loved (so he says) the Church and you
Doretta loved, sought only love's full fruit:
And Haydn loved, was but importunate:
And you loved, dear, was but obedient:
We all of us were loving, were we not?
Yet working outward, wisely, as we deem'd,
We all have done that which we would undo. —
Tell me now, who has tamper'd with these deeds?
I do believe, though I have doubted it,
There is a devil! Hell-scorch'd hands alone
Could weave such blacken'd shrouds from these
bright threads
Drawn from sleek skeins of love. That spider foul,
Feeding on our sweet plans, emits this web,

To trip and trap us in like flies! — Ah me,
It may be well that one should suffer here
Until his wish bereaved shriek prayers for death;
But through what fearful pangs earth saps, earth peels
This withering flesh off from the worthier soul.
The scales about my life grow thin, how thin!
Johanna, Haydn gone, home gone, hope gone,
What further shred invests this spirit stript! —
My soul, thou art enthrall'd from earth. Look, look!
Yet where is heaven? — My God, I see it not."

"O father, rave not thus," I cried. "O, if —
If Haydn, — if I had some power with him." —

"Nay, daughter," said he, "nay." Yet o'er his face
Flush'd hope like sunrise; and I kiss'd his brow:
"Yes, father, I will try," and went my way.

When I found Haydn then, he was so sad.
"Ah," sigh'd he, "we two souls seem'd fitted so
To match each other. In this jarring world,
Where all goes contrary, where every sun
Which ripes this withers that; and every storm

Which brings refreshment here, sends deluge there,
We two, exceptions to the general rule,
Like living miracles (is love fulfill'd
A miracle indeed?) seem'd form'd to draw
The self-same tale of weal or woe from each.
Dear, in my dreams, but last night I beheld
Our spirits journeying through this under gloom;
And they walk'd hand in hand; and over them,
As over limner'd seraphs, there did hang
A halo, love reflected. By its glow
The gloom about wax'd brightness; and, far off,
In clearest lines, the path pass'd up and on.—
Johanna, heed me, once again, I pray,
[If ever I did pray to God above]
Blot not all light from my eternity!"

"Haydn," I answer'd, "would you have me change?
What one shall dwell upon God's holy hill
But 'he that sweareth to his own hurt,' yes,
'And changeth not?'"

"But," he replied, "but yet
If you were wrong to swear? How can it be
That any course unnatural, like this,
Is right? Each instinct of my soul revolts."

"Yet nature," said I, "it may be corrupt.
What is this instinct, that it should not lie?
If one should feel the instinct of the lamb
While skipping to welcome the butcher's knife
That waits to slaughter it, would he be wise
To follow such?"

"And why not?" answer'd he;
"The lamb was made that it might die for man:
It follows instinct and dies easily.
The soul was made that it might live for God:
It follows instinct and lives happily.
The cases differ thus. May there not be
Some sphere, beyond the watch of mortal eye,
Within whose subtle grooves our spirits glide
Unconscious of the balancings of will?
God's Spirit is too holy to be seen.
May it not stir, beneath all conscious powers,
A spontaneity which moves the soul
As instinct moves the body? — Ah, to me,
Love seems an instinct which impels them both."

"How so?" I ask'd, hoping to guide his thought
Toward sacrifice.

"Do you wish me," he said,
"To turn philosopher for you? — Well, then,
This love, in morals sprung from faith in man,
And in religion sprung from faith in God,
Is, in its essence, an experience
Not wholly feeling yet not wholly thought,
Not all of body yet not all of soul,
Of what we are or of what we shall be,
But more akin to marriage, within self,
Of our constituent natures, sense and soul.
God meant them to be join'd: when wedded thus,
This rests contented, and that waits in hope."

"To rest, to wait," I said to this; "and if
Such ends were displaced would there not remain
Work? Is not work our earthly heritage?"

"And may not God," rejoin'd he, "grant us more
Than that which we inherit?"

I replied, —
"He may grant rest. Yet rest, the Paradise
Of work, is still the Purgatory, too,
Of indolence."

HAYDN.

"The soul's true Paradise
Is nothing earn'd," he said. "It is a gift.
With Eden lost, insolvent for his sin,
Work, as I view it, is a loan from Hope
With which man pays the debt of Memory.
But if I reckon right, he scarce can earn
Enough to pay both Memory and Hope.
So true love, as I view it, is a gift
Crowning our action, yet not won by it;
Which, as we are not conscious how 'tis earn'd,
We are not conscious how it may be lost.
Things out of consciousness are out of care.
We rest not as in death, which doeth naught:
We rest as in our dreams, in sleep, — a life
In which God watches while the soul regales.
We rest not from the healthful stir of work,
But from the slavery proportioning
Our pleasure to our pain, — a law for serfs,
But not for sons. Such rest is peaceful, hush'd,
The very church of choice, as different
From other joy as prayer is from sport."

"And choice, feels it no sacred claim," I ask'd,
"To spurn a lesser for a higher good?
Or, for such good, may not wise Providence
Displace some idol of our ignorance?" —

With this, I pictured for him brightest life;
And, like a blot upon each scene, myself;
Urged that my character was not the one
Form'd most to succor his; show'd how my sire,
The priest, Doretta, all agreed in this.
And then, in contrast with myself, I sketch'd
One whom they all deem'd fitted for his moods.
I may have sinn'd in it; but, like grim fate,
My father's features seem'd to impel me on:
I noted all Doretta's noblest traits;
Then, when I thought that he must this surmise,
And while he held his gaze upon the floor,
As though he gave assent, at last I spake
Doretta's name.

And if the solid earth
Had quak'd, he had not started more. O God,
Why did I not accept his instinct then!

He look'd at me, first pale, then flush'd, then griev'd;
Then with strange, tremulous, painful breath, he said, —
"And this device from you? You were so pure,
So free from guile. You should have spared me this.

That Jesuit has train'd you well! Ah, now,
I know how Adam felt when Eve did fall;
How Eve herself, when round her soul first crept
The serpent's cautious coils of smooth deceit,
Smothering by inches. I can read it now,
That tale: it is an allegory, aye;—
That serpent is the world. The world steals round,
Encircling childhood, trammeling it from heaven.
Not long are we allow'd ideal life,
Not long unfetter'd sense or unbound heart:
Our smiles grow stiffer, till, some fatal day,
The last one clutch'd, is held, a horrid grin.
Then, when the body stirs not with the soul,
The last nerve sever'd from the spirit's touch,
Naught in us left to love, the world unwinds:
Our capturer, it dissolves in mist or dust:—
For its embraces we have lost our God!"

His mood alarm'd me, yet I could protest,—
"Haydn, you know I do not love this world:—
I long to leave it, yes, all thought of it."

"How much less worldliness," ask'd he, "deem you
Found in the Church than in what it terms world?
The prince of this world is not nice in choice

Of equipages; where he cannot check
He mounts the car of truth and grasps the rein;
And if the devil drive, he drives toward home.
'The world,' what means it but the mere world,
Matter devoid of mind and things of truth?—
What means, what has your Church?—A court of priests
Powerful through personal friendship with each knave,
Heart-husbands of all disaffected wives,
Preachers, the very prostitutes of truth,
Aye pregnant by each latest prejudice.—
'The world' means human action without God.
What has your Church?—Worship where He is hid
Behind strange saints enthroned! adored through rites
Of wolves robed in the pure white of the lamb.
Devils disguised, 'mid ceremonious cant
Tempting into hypocrisy an age
Which knows too much of Christianity
To be tempted into heathenism. Nay,
I will not stop.— 'The world' means human life
Without the Christ-like manhood meant for man.
What has your Church?—These nurseries of death!
God's beauteous bodies rotted in damp cells,
Where His sun steals not save to stir vile stench!
Life, cursed with this damnation from a vow
Which He hath not enjoin'd;—to make a hell

Of what He meant for heaven; to feel no love
Except with some foul consciousness of sin!
Life, where imprison'd nature, gone insane,
Rapes in its morbid mood all virtuous rest;
And stains with dregs of stagnant viciousness
The open'd cells of pure, pure hearts like yours!"

"You terrify me, Haydn!" I exclaim'd.

"And you have terrified me," he rejoin'd.
"You were — Ah me, what were you not? — so pure,
Transparent as this mid-day atmosphere.
Should some red thunderbolt burst from yon sun
And burn all torturing blindness through both eyes,
Night came less unexpected! I, who dream'd
That I did worship truth, that these proud knees
Knelt on the very battlements of heaven,
I, to be tript thus from dear confidence,
Sent reeling down amid this foul deceit,
Is it a wonder if scared sense be jarr'd
Out of all order, if I rave, if curse! —
You, who had known my heart; and, after that,
And after I had warn'd against the thing,
And simulating all the while such love,
Of free will, calmly, meanly, cunningly,

Vowing thus to abjure me: more than this,
To-day, with cat-like, treacherous approach,
Sneaking through secret doorways left ajar
By too frank intimacy, entering
The inmost chambers of my love, to snare
Your victim for a shrew!—It is success!
You gain your end! My wish is yours, at last!
I love you not!—God help!—You may go free!"

Then Haydn would have left our home in haste;
From which my sire restrain'd him. Long they
spake:
And loud and stormy were the words he used.
But then, at last, my father told him all,—
Why I had vow'd, that I might save his life.
And he broke down before it.

Never more
May God permit me to behold again
A broken man! How he did plead with me!
He begg'd, he pray'd forgiveness o'er and o'er,
Till I well-nigh believ'd he heard me not;
And in the end sigh'd that "It might be so,"
My plan be wisest;—nay, he did not yield
His stronger judgment, to fulfill my wish
Or make me happy, or my sire or me:—

Truly Doretta was a housewife wise:
It was the older custom, thus to wed:
He had been young, had whims: — God bless us
all."

Oft after that I urged him not to wed
Except one whom he loved. And he would say,
"I cannot love her, dear, as I love you: —
Yet what if not? My soul was immature,
Wean'd romance late. It must be manly now.
Manhood has breadth. I take it, manly love
Is that which yields most blessings to the most.
My love shall bless you, and the sire, and her." —
And thus he calm'd my doubts, and cheer'd me
much.

And oft I spake with him about the Church.
"I love the truth," he said; "as for the Church, —
How can my heart forget that it holds you?"

"Haydn," rejoin'd I, "I remember once
When you were small, when first sweet music lured
Your soul, so thrill'd! to test its energies:
Gluck was your master, and you worshipt him,
So far beyond yourself, as you then deem'd,

Sounded the full perfection of his strains.
Now Gluck is not your master; yet, far off,
Still sound those perfect strains for which you
strive. —
Haydn, you only saw Gluck in the path,
Happening to be in front. But ah, those strains? —
You will not reach them, dearest, till you reach
The choirs of God!

"And thus, sometimes, I think
That I, too, may have happen'd in your path.
This love of yours, now resting on myself,
May gaze for holier things, ideal all,
When I am gone."

"When you are gone!" he sigh'd,
"When you are gone, then shall my life become —
I fear it much — one lonely wail for you."

"And yet a lonely wail, utter'd," I said,
"From some sweet, chasten'd spirit, may seem sweet
To earth that hears it."

"Ah, I understand.
You mean my music," answer'd he. "O God,

Must love be sacrific'd that art be saved?—
Redeem'd at such a price, it were too dear!"

One thing he promis'd me. I urged it much.
"In secret convent-prayers," I said to him,
"My soul must know if it should praise or plead.
A year from this day will we meet once more.
It were not wise to speak. We shall commune
While I gaze, silent, through my cloister-bars.
Then, if your wedded life afford you joy—
As I doubt not—bring me fresh buds, fresh flowers;
If otherwise, bring me the wilted leaves
Of these I give you now."

Soon they had pass'd,
The last vague hours which saw me part from all.
I stood before the shrine. I feel it yet:—
The organ wildly moaning far away:
The people sighing deeply through the aisles:
My heart so loud in that hush'd sermon-time:
The multitude with eyes so fix'd on me;
My sire's sad face; Doretta by his side;
And Haydn's face upon his pale, pale hands.

And two months after that I saw them wed.
And, sister, I have pray'd for him long days,

And longer nights; and I have had large hopes
That my faint spirit had gain'd strength from God.
But my poor body here, so white, so thin,
With scarce substantiality of guise
Fit for a ghost; — ah, what if, like a ghost,
It should soon vanish?

So I thought, to-night,
If I could tell you all; confess this fault;
Unload my heart of its sin — its sweet sin,
That God might give it ease. I did not, nay,
I did not mean it, to excite myself.
They told me that it might bring death; but O,
Have I not done enough to merit peace?
How I had counted time, these weeks and days,
Up to the hour when we should meet again,
And I should find out that my prayers were heard,
And that God had been kind!

And Haydn came,
Last week: and, sister, what, what does God mean? —
He brought the wilted leaves.

I do not know.
I only know that I cannot earn peace:

All our whole household have earn'd so much else!
And now, how can — I can try nothing more:
But all my path has been block'd up, block'd up.
They tell me this is infidelity, —
O Christ! — yet I can do no more.

Hark! hark! —
Is not that Haydn's melody again? —
How faint it sounds! I think I must be faint. —
The window — move me. There — look out — those
clouds —
Sunset? — There are no things on earth so bright
So beautiful as clouds; and yet no clouds
Where one could see, and always see, the heaven.

The music, hear it! Ah, how sweet! — Tell me,
Did I sing then? — "No"? — Did I only dream? —
I thought that music mine, mine and myself;
And Haydn's heart, it beat here, beat in me. —
I am so tired. — Yes: let me rest on you.
O God, for but one hour of life! — For what?
Have I not loved then? — Sister, tell him so,
Tell Haydn; thank him. — God, praise Him for it.
I did not know — yet life, it has been sweet. —
Hark! music! — Does it not come from above?

LYRICAL POEMS.

THE IDEALIST.

FANCY is term'd a fickle guide
  Of rarest birth and beauty,
But all too heavenly to abide
  In earth bereft of duty.
    When up the sky
    Her bright wings hie
So far above all worldly fears,
When o'er her airy course appears
  About the welkin wended
  Full many a spirit splendid,
Beware! amid all sunny air
The storm may burst, the lightning tear.
    Beware and fear!
    With earth so near
  None can be free from care.

Fancy is term'd a fooling guide,
  All smiles when one is youthful,
But wont in sudden shades to hide,
  And prove at last untruthful.
    Man is but man:
    He cannot scan

Too high delights; or he may hate
The pleasures of his low estate.
  When down to earth far falling,
  Amid dismay, recalling
Her realm, her idle realm of dreams,
See, how with reckless rival gleams
    The daze unreal,
    The void ideal
  Pales life's substantial themes.

Fancy is term'd a fulsome guide
  Who renders life distressful,
Far too ethereal in her pride
  To make a man successful.
    Along her way
    Let poets stray:
Earth only shoos or shoots a bird;
To draw its wealth, it yokes the herd.
  Few are our race respecting
  The minds for aye projecting.
The reigning heroes of the day
Among the plodding people stay;
    Note well the tide
    On either side,
  But keep the common way.

Yet fickle, fooling, fulsome guide,
  I prize thy peerless beauty.
I chose thee long ago, my bride
  For love and not for booty.
    What have they wrought
    Who hazard naught?
What care I though the best of bliss
May border on the worst abyss?
  What, though this world may never
  Believe me good or clever?—
Enough it is, for me to know
That truth right righteously may flow
    From thee and me
    Till braver be
  The faith of friend and foe.

THE DESTINY-MAKER.

SHE pass'd; and I who linger'd there,
I saw that she was very fair;
And, with my sighs that pride suppress'd,
Flutter'd a weary wish for rest.
    But I who had resolv'd to be
    The maker of my destiny,
    I turn'd me to my task and wrought,
    And so forgot the passing thought.

She paused; and I who question'd there,
I heard she was as good as fair;
And in my soul a still, small voice
Did chide because I check'd my choice.
    But I, who had resolv'd to be
    The maker of my destiny,
    I bade the gentle guardian down,
    And tried to think about renown.

She left; and I who wander, fear
There's nothing more to see or hear;

Those walls that ward my Paradise
Are very high, nor open twice.
    And I, who had resolv'd to be
    The maker of my destiny,
    Can only wait without the gate
    And sit and sigh — Too late! too late!

CAGED.

THE jest and gossip ceas'd at last:
It seem'd as though my lips were fast.
Ah me, such holy hopes loom'd then
My mind could only think amen.
But soon she cried out, "How absurd!"
And laugh'd, whereat her little bird
Took up the music of the word,
And trill'd an echo, loud and long,
Till, deafen'd quite, we still'd the song.

"That bird," said she, "hush! hush!" and sigh'd,
"Flew in the door one Whitsun-tide.
I caught and caged, and soon he grew
The sweetest pet you ever knew:
Lights on my finger, in my hair,
And pecks my lips: 'twould make you stare
To see with what a jaunty air
He drags a tiny cart I made,
And plays parade and cannonade.

"One day, last spring, he flew away.
Alas! you should have seen the way
We wept for him, and search'd the town;
And how it made the neighbors frown
The twentieth time we ask'd for him.
But last we spied him on that limb
Close by the house. 'Twas dusk, quite dim,
But I call'd out, and back he flew:
Did n't you birdie? naughty you!"

With this, once more she laugh'd at him.
And I, — I thought the room grew dim,
And then, I whisper'd, "Dear, a word, —
I know one other little bird
That longs so much to fly to you;
And, dearest, you may cage it too:
'Twill sing and serve and be so true!"
And then she blush'd, and then she wept,
And then this bird of love she kept.

THE HIGHEST CLAIM.

I WOKE and said: The night has gone;
  And gone each eager guest
Whose urgency, from dark to dawn,
  Distracted dreams of rest.
One styled me prince; one warrior grand;
  One tempted me with gold;
One held a scroll, and bade my hand
  A pen immortal hold.
But each spake naught of Him who wrought,
  My soul, the most for me:
  And He hath higher claim on thee.

To hold the sceptre of the State,
  Like Moses, o'er that sea
Where rival forces strive with fate
  And fail of victory?—
Ah no, high up, above the rod
  Man's feeble arm sustains,
The never tiring hand of God
  All earthly power ordains.
He on the throne who reigns alone,
  My soul, thy Lord must be;
  For He hath higher claim on thee.

To wield a sword in warful times
  Till foes yield up each aim,
While Hope with eager footstep climbs
  The trembling heights of fame?—
Ah no, though all earth far and wide
  Should echo loud my name,
The fame thus won might not out-bide
  The brief success of shame.
A name sublime that bides all time,
  My soul, thou canst foresee;
  And it hath higher claim on thee.

To join the throngs whose toils have told
  Of wealth so dear to sight,
And dearer than the gleaming gold
  Of earth by it made bright?—
Ah no, these treasures mined from earth
  Lure down toward deeper gloom:
There is a gleam from higher worth
  Hangs, star-like, o'er the tomb:
A peerless goal, a sinless soul,
  My soul, thou mayest be;
  And that hath higher claim on thee.

With my own lips to rouse the life
  Of laggard victory,

Or with my pen to sketch the strife
  Of ages yet to be?—
'Twill not suffice while there may sound
  A voice more dear from man
Than music marshaling in its round
  This world far down the van:
A strain so dear God rests to hear,
  My soul, with love the key,
  This,—this hath higher claim on thee.

Ah, why through all life's little day
  Should cannon roar and trumpet call,
And cluster'd smoke from many a fray
  Hang o'er one like a pall?—
Small is the space above the fight
  This rolling thunder jars;
The echoes sleep in paths of light
  Where move eternal stars.
To lead toward love, aye calm above,
  My soul, thy work may be;
  Let this have highest claim on thee.

I spake: and while full light of dawn
  Bedimm'd my eyes, each guest
That I had thought for aye had gone
  Return'd and hail'd me blest.

One styled me prince; one, warrior grand;
  One open'd stores of gold;
One held a scroll, and bade my hand
  A pen immortal hold:
And, with one voice, all cried, "Thy choice,
  O soul, its wisdom see! —
  It, too, hath highest claim on me."

THE WEDDING DAY.

THOU rarest flower that life hath grown,
  Day bursting now from bulb of night,
To more ambrosial blushing blown
  Shed not for aye thy leaves of light
    Still fresh perennially.

Attendant winds, ye drowsy airs,
  Breathe hence, intoxicate with sweets;
Exhale delight to gathering cares
  Till aged love with ardor greets
    Dawn from eternity.

Clouds, if ye must come, lightly rest
  As birds that float a shadeless sky,
That crowd mild winds in wild contest,
  Then under arbors dive and lie
    Deep-laved in minstrelsy.

Sun, bid these rays shine on, through life,
  Aurora o'er the blackest night,
A bow above the clouds of strife,
  A glory gilding robes of flight
    O'er Love's last victory.

MY IDEAL.

SHE came: she went: 'twas but a dream,
  A groundless hope, a fruitless scheme;
And yet the dearest dream did seem
  That ere to mortal gaze was given.
She tuned sweet music through my breast
Till every sad or joyous guest
That long had sway'd, with wondering rest,
  Grew silent as grow sins in heaven.

She came: she went: a beam sublime
Which, straying toward a sunless clime,
Trembled along the edge of Time
  And then in fright sped back again.
Ah, wherefore came if came to go!
I had not known the half of woe
Had I not felt that heavenly glow,
  And, match'd with it, found earth so vain.

She came: she went: I know I dream'd,
Nor dared to test fond hopes that gleam'd;

But yet how dear the future seem'd,
  And, though it was the world, how real!
Ah, wherefore did she leave so soon,
And change to night what might be noon:
Did Heaven sufficient deem the boon
  To grant to me a form ideal?

THE MUSIC OF LIFE.

MUSIC round the world is sounding,
  Sweeter than e'er heard by man,
Music angel hosts surrounding
  Ere the morning stars began;
Sweeter than dear dreams of music,
  Falling softer on the ear
Than the footfalls of far echoes
  Treading o'er the midnight-meer,
Thrilling more than martial anthems,
  Or the gleams of long lost hope,
More enticing than the sunbeams
  Wooing dew from plain and slope,
Sacred strains, and rival'd only
  Where those trembling tones control
When the touch of ardor holy
  Stirs sweet sighing from the soul.

Music round the world beginning,
  Low-attuning night and day,
Wheresoe'er the worlds are spinning
  Sweeter swells in many a lay.

In each heart, howe'er forsaken,
  When these cheering notes resound,
Slumbering joy again must waken,
  Thrilling up from depths profound;
And once more make light its beating,
  Till, like hosts at morning drum,
Life, from each roused artery meeting,
  Bounding through the pulses, come.
Heard by inward senses only,
  Blessed boon from realms above,
Life of life and order holy,
  Breathes the still small voice of love.

NOTES FROM THE VICTORY.

AH me, who is ringing those bells?
  Right merry for funeral knells!
If wild winds fell ring them through hell,
  What woe can the demons lack?
My light blew out, in the gust of the rout:
  My boy will never come back.

  Drums, too, — who bade the drums roll?
  Coarse drums, call ye the soul?
Folks out of breath, shout ye at death?
  Rend ye the tomb? — Alack,
Vain echoes around, still, under the ground,
  My boy can never come back.

  And guns! — What makes the guns roar!
  Alas, I thought it was o'er!
Though why fear I, though millions die,
  Though all of us wear but black?
I, too, with the proud have my blood-stain'd shroud
    My boy will never come back.

Our land! — who wants its long years?
  They are dimm'd by these drainless tears:
All gloom is the way of this mourner gray
  Who groans in their lonely track.
Chill, shivering breast, freeze, freeze into rest.
  My boy can never come back.

OCCASIONAL AND DESCRIPTIVE POEMS.

OUR DAY AT PISA.

WE took the train at Florence, we:
  The day was mild and pleasant.
The town of Pisa we would see,
  And buy a "Parian" present.
We coursed the streets, and climb'd the tower;
Dropt something down, and sat an hour;
And then the grand baptistry door
Swung wide for us and half a score.
But soon we tired; heard o'er and o'er,
  Its echo grew provoking.

We made our pockets jingle, we,
  To tempt the cicerone;
Saw the cathedral, paid the fee,
  And ate some macaroni.
Then feasted on an outside view
Of those three buildings, still so new:
Then sought the Campo Santo, more
Because we must; and, last, a store,
Where, treating each gift like a bore,
  We screw'd it in our cloaking.

We took the train at sunset, we,
And, as we left the station,
Talk'd of the land, "How much to see!
How grand the Roman nation!
Our own, how mean! — no works of art."
Both sigh'd at this. Then, with a start,
Cried, "How familiar!" o'er and o'er,
In joy recalling themes of yore —
No hint from art: we heard once more
A frog near by us croaking.

THE ORIGIN OF DRESS.

ONCE came the devil in a serpent's mien
To fold in his embrace earth's eldest queen;
And she was snared soon, being still quite young,
By such a pliant air and ready tongue.
Then Adam came, whereat the serpent fled,
But all too quickly save his skin to shed.
Eve could but blush, yet, taught deceit the while,
The coils call'd hoops — which thence became the style —
And swore, she blush'd to see her Adam nude.
Since which hath dress been deem'd, wherever view'd,
Enough redress for all like turpitude.

THE BURNING OF THE CHURCH AT SANTIAGO.

In 1864 the Immaculate Conception of the Virgin was celebrated with unusual splendor in the Church de la Companiè of Santiago, Chili. During the ceremonies the draped image of the Virgin caught fire. Almost instantly, the flames were communicated to ropes suspending along the ceiling upward of twenty thousand colored lamps. These fell in a rain of fire upon the audience below, and a scene of horror followed which beggars description. As many as two thousand persons, chiefly young ladies from the higher grades of society, perished beneath the ruins.

O'ER Santiago's joyous home
  The setting sun delay'd,
And high on one uplifted dome
  A second sunset made.
And thitherward the old and young
  Came thronging through each street;
And many a thought tript o'er the tongue
  To match their merry feet.
"This night," they cried, "God's blessed bride,
  Is praised in earth and heaven.
All we shall bow before her now,
  With all our sins forgiven.

"Blaze forth those twenty thousand lights!
  Blaze shields and standards bright!
Blaze saints and seraphs thron'd in heights
  That dim the dazzled sight!
Wild wake the surging minstrelsy!
  Wave incense richly rare!
Our hearts shall trill the harmony
  And float in spirit-air!
Full well we know, while brightly glow
  These splendid honors given,
How pleased are they to whom we pray
  To see such sights from heaven.

"Hush! down to Mary mother bow —
  Why not to Mary's mother?
That frowning Christ shall heed one now —
  Strange how he own'd a brother!
What's that? — lit up? — how queer a flame!
  Our Matron saint on fire?
O holy Mother, look!" — "For shame! —
  It does not fright the friar. —
Keep still, keep still: I count but ill; —
  God knows how I have striven: —
Down on your knees; — such prayers as these! —
  You'll never be forgiven."

Blazed all those twenty thousand lamps;
  Blazed saints and seraphs bright.
O God! the close cathedral cramps:—
  Dear penance paid to-night!
Death's fiery hand shrimpt badge and band,
  And wrapt the dimming dome.
Down hot as hell the red lamps fell
  To fright their victims home.
Wild woke a wail: "The door! To fail?—
  O Mary, hear from heaven!"—
No more, no more shall swing that door:—
  All lost or all forgiven.

That demon, Death, came sweeping down
  And touch'd each maiden's cheek;
They blush'd; but, O, with blush too brown!
  They kneel'd; but, O, too meek!
He wrapt them round with robes of flame:
  He crimpt their waving hair;
And, when their souls were won, he came
  And scoopt them through the air.
Anon the fire is tossing higher:
  The church is calm as heaven;
Save bells that tell a last farewell,
  Far down the steeple driven.

O'er Santiago's mourning home
  The morning sunbeams stray'd,
And found — ah, not that gleaming dome,
  Nor many a bright-eyed maid ; —
Four hundred carts of corpses charr'd,
  Two thousand nameless dead,
And scores of thousands weeping hard
  For souls and splendor fled.
But these alive, these who survive,
  May they not draw near heaven ?
With humbled calls from brown burnt walls,
  May they not be forgiven ?

Yes, ye who gaze aloft with fear
  And conscience-crushing pain,
It is not God will sooner hear
  The saint with splendid train.
Each gilded arch and architrave,
  All earth must burn some day :
The guide to save beyond the grave
  Is Christ, who proved the way.
The simplest prayer is welcome where
  Our sovereign Lord of heaven
Is one who cried, when crucified, —
  All finish'd, all forgiven.

SAINT PETER.

ALTERED FROM AN ANCIENT LEGEND.

THE night before his crucifixion, Peter stole
Out from the prison-walls which long had barr'd his soul
From Christian fellowship and labor. Fast he sped
Through dusky lawns and lanes whither a forest spread
Its trembling shades to screen him. Thence there gleam'd a light,
A welcoming window from the home of friends. Not quite
Had he reach'd this when, open'd by the rounded moon,
Deep vales reveal'd the city towers, grand as at noon.
Then first awoke full consciousness that he was free;
And falling on his knees, he cried in tears, "To Thee,
To Thee, O Christ, be all the praise!" He paused. He thought

He heard soft footfalls nearing him. In fear he sought
Their source; when, lo! far off, on rocks too rough for moss,
And tottering beneath his brown and blood stain'd cross,
The well-known form of his Redeemer. Seeing Him,
No longer Peter fear'd; but leap'd with eager limb
Across sharp crags, as once ere this across the sea,
Calling in joyous tones: "O, Lord, I come to Thee!"
He moved in vain. The vision drew back in thin air.
Then Peter sat him down and wept. But, through despair,
A small voice whisper'd, "Peter, wouldst thou come to me,
Go hence: do for the world as I have done for thee."
One moment Peter linger'd; then resought the plain,
And ere the morrow's noon his soul had met his Lord again.

AMID THE MOUNTAINS.

MY mountains, how I love you as ye stand,
So beautiful, so bleak, so grim, so grand!
Yon gleaming crags above my boyhood's play
Undimm'd as hope hung o'er each dawning day.
Now, when light-burden'd hope gives place to care,
O'er steadfast toil I see you steadfast there.
And when old age would scan its heavenly way,
Its glance shall rest refresh'd upon those summits
gray.

Ah, beautiful, too beautiful for truth,
Your landscapes lured my wistful eyes in youth.
Now, when rude hands those earlier views assail,
When towns and cities change the lower vale;
When other friends seem lost or sadly strange,
Ye stand familiar still; ye do not change.
And ye alone, where this my life is o'er,
Rise past all views of Time, the self-same ever-
more.

Mounts, ye deserve it, flushing first when dawn
Reveals new gleams of truth o'er night withdrawn,

Still rear your regal rustics, first who vow
To serve the serf and brand the despot's brow.
In marsh, in mead, if tyrants make men mild,
The slaves who scale your sides learn winds are
wild;
That beasts break loose from bonds, that fowls are
free:
And tired fear rests to wake 'mid dreams of liberty.

High homes of freedom, earth no voice can raise
So strong, so full, to echo half your praise.
By Waldus' church, and Ziska's liberty,
By Swiss and Scot who named their nations free,
By my New England, when she call'd him knave,—
The lowland foe who chased his flying slave,
Stand as their memory, forever grand!
They lordliest of the race, ye heavenliest of the
land.

Would ye might stand, eternal monuments
Of those who proved Truth's noblest precedents.
But no: they need you not! As bright as right,
Their spirits were belied! O, snowy white.
Their stations lower'd! O, summits less sublime.
They aim'd at stars to feed the hopes of Time;
And, when worlds waste and mountains cease to be,
'Mid holier heights than ye, shall thrive eternally.

WITH THE YOUNG.

HARSH contact with the world, I know,
  Is a blessing when withstood:
Its victor's sword has the brightest glow,
  And its conqueror conquers good.
Yet not for age, when naught confines,
  Do my first feelings well;
To younger life my love inclines,
  And with the young I dwell.

Why ask a feeling the reason why?—
  My lot may have been too hard;
Some woe from whisper'd fears on high
  May weigh the hope of reward:
Life knows that many, too many fall
  Whose steps all deem'd secure:
It fears that none can trip at all
  And ever again be pure.

Perchance, through each sweet childish face
  Speaks some one loved of yore,

Some distant life whose deeds I trace
  Beside me here no more,
Some soul now in eternity,
  Where still, as thought maintains,
What is, what has been, what shall be,
  In changeless state remains.

Perchance I share in heaven's delight
  O'er memories of the past,
Or in the saints who guide, at night,
  Earth's children through the blast: —
But leave the cause still undivin'd,
  When thoughts the freëst well,
The young have claims none others find,
  And with the young I dwell.

DIDACTIC POEMS.

OF SUCH IS THE KINGDOM OF HEAVEN.

WHAT has a child that a man has not
When of such is the kingdom of heaven?
Behold him, in harness of home and of school,
Not a whit does he care for the right of a rule
When enough of recess is given.
He frolics in freedom of wild desires,
Of fancy that rushes and reels and tires.
His limbs, they leap and fidget and throw,
Nor ever think that is the way to grow.
His words are fickle, like waves of a brook,
A-spatter or smooth to answer the crook.
All things on earth that are fair to see,
Are sweet to attract as flowers to a bee.
What virtue is his?—While man, he could read
Of God every day and question His deed,
The child bears still the stamp of the skies,
A faith that he has not learn'd to despise,
Expression that knows no other control
Than that of the Maker who moves the soul,
A beauty of wisdom that works to obey
A holy, because a natural way:
And that has a child that a man may have not.

What has a man that a child has not
When traces of heaven are rare?
O, he has been taught by parents and schools
To curb his character in by rules
Till nothing but rules are there.
The childless man, he would spurn to find
What God designs the quest of his mind.
He crams and drams for an appetite
That pales the simple and shocks the right.
His words are dry, as the words of a book;
You turn your sentence wherever you look.
His thoughts — he never saw anything strange:
If he did some fellow might doubt his range.
And all of the truth he tests by pelf,
And all of manhood measures by self,
Forgets that God made the life he is at
And stars himself as its autocrat.
Alas for reason with such a judge!
If ever you whisper or wheeze or budge,
You may study and ponder and prove and pray,
But he has a disagreeable way:
And that may he have that a child has not.

What has a man that a child has too
When of such is the kingdom of heaven?
He knows that character mends through rules,
But knows of the split 'twixt the wise and the fools,

The choice of the ruling given.
He feels that the worth of a life proceeds
From Him who prompted the bent of deeds.
He lets the reins of his being go
Wherever the soul moves wisely so.
He trusts in God through self and his Book,
Or pointing the way through a bishop's crook,
But he welcomes the merit of that which is new,
Nor dreams all Christendom Timbuctoo;
For modest he is, and loves to find
Earth bless'd by moods of a differing kind.
In short, to the simple, the frail, and the true,
He is just a republican, through and through;
And, waving your reason its right of control,
Trusts God for enough truth left in your soul;
And though he may differ, and doubt your way,
He has something to love in spite of his nay:
And that may a man and a child have too.

NOTHING TO KEEP UNDER.

YOU envy, friend, what love will greet
  With never failing favors,
The work, the word, the wish discreet
  That ne'er of passion savors,
The mien no blow of insult swerves
  From aptitude to blunder,
A stouter something o'er the nerves
  Or less nerves to keep under.

You envy, friend, compliant thought
  With passing currents shifting,
Quick turn'd by windy words that wrought
  Its light attention lifting,
Whose welcome hints no half-check'd heed
  Of woe or wrath or wonder
To feel how hard is life indeed
  With so much to keep under.

You envy, friend, contented moods
  That crave no explorations,

Steer clear, no matter what intrudes,
  And risk no observations;
That cause no self-occasion'd strife
  Where breakers wildly thunder,
But hold a cautious helm to life
  And keep temptation under.

You envy, friend, — but O, maybe,
  True power is bred from meekness,
And strength that grows through mastery
  May be the ward of weakness;
Who learns to rule your headstrong soul
  May earn a sway fecunder
Than struggling less, with more control, —
  But nothing to keep under.

TO AN ARTIST.

IN candor, my friend, you seem too much at home
With gods of Olympus and maids of old Rome.
The world has advanced; and the artist, if sage,
Will seek to embody the thoughts of his age.
The curve of a limb and the poise of a head
May be all the same in the living as dead;
But the fashion of form is the fit of a frame:
In art, as in action, seek merit in aim.

Truth only is lasting: where fame has long youth
Those nearest immortal are nearest to truth:
They sketch from the present, its deeds and its dreams,
As Raphael wrought, but not Raphael's themes.
You are no Venetian to temper like Titian
A woman to worship or goddess to kiss:
You are a new-world's man; model from this.

So long I have hoped that the sons of the band
Who have limner'd the loveliest views of our land

Would let the dead bury their dead, and pursue
The life of the future, the love of the new:
The proudest ambition, the readiest hand,
Might wisely court ideals less grand;
No sweeter Murillo's divinest designs,
Where purity rivals the thought it refines,
And the dreamy intent of a life-brooding haze
Throngs thick with the beauty of immature praise;
No nobler the types that the Spaniard could scan,
Inspired to incarnate a soul in each plan,
The life of a picture as well as of man.

Instead, I find customs stript to assuage
The heathenish tastes of a heathenish age;
The dead unearth'd, the more filth to find vent,
The more dear to each dog-of-an-amateur's scent;
Thin, shoddy-spun sentiment, sleek to the crude,
About art, as all pure, in spite of "the prude:"
Yet if influence be a test of a deed,
And ill be handled that ill succeed,
The naked device of an impure art
Is the foulest of all things having no heart:
Mount vice on a monument, viler below
The vicious will gloat, and the virtuous go.

In truth, my friend, I think to the wise
That beauty seems best which is best for all eyes:

And in faces and forms which all classes befriend
The true and the good, with the beautiful, blend.

Besides, in all action is one test of worth —
The soul that wins homage must benefit earth.
But I fear, with an eye fixt alone on the old,
With the world that has been alone for a mold,
While the world that shall be can alone elevate,
That the vice of all vice is to imitate.
Ah, rather find form for Faith's purest ideal,
The world shall be blest while it fancies it real.
Small virtue has he with no hope in his heart;
Small merit has he with no hope in his art;
Far nobler a hoosier-man modestly wary,
Content with his photograph-glimpse of a prairie.

ON RAPHAEL'S ANGELS.

I WONDER not that artists' hands,
  Inspired by themes of joy,
Presuming forms of angel-bands,
  Are moved to paint the boy.

I know if task to me were given
  To woo desires of men
By that in earth the nearest heaven,
  Most dear to mortal ken,

I would not take thee, O my bride!
  For some brides are no gain;
Nor him with influence his pride,
  For more than right can reign;

No matron with her life confined
  To partial thoughts of youth:
No sire with all his warp of mind
  Closed tight to outer truth:

But I would blend the purity
  Of her whom I adore,
With manly power for mastery
  And promise still in store.

So I would take the boy who roams
  Toward life half understood
From thresholds of those holy homes
  Which face alone the good:

His station, ere he reach'd that brink
  Where vice must cross his track,
While wish that loathes the wish to drink
  Still keeps the tempter back:

His spirit, innocent of ill,
  Or sense to apprehend,
With cheeks that blush, with eyes that fill,
  And faith that fears no end.

And O, I know that those who love
  The purest part of joys,
Would choose but one from all above,
  And that, — my heaven of boys.

THE COUNTRY-COUSIN'S QUESTION.

IF one would have his friendship sought,
  Would please the world appealing,
Should he have head with less of thought,
  Or heart with less of feeling?

Can it be that suspicions wait
  On words that are sincerest,
Can open frankness be a gate
  To close, and then seem dearest?

Or does such sin pervade our youth
  And so much flippant folly,
That all the wise should smother truth,
  Joyous or melancholy,

Till art alone seem natural,
  This night of Nature haunting
To make deception general
  Where charity is wanting?

WHATEVER THE MISSION OF LIFE MAY BE.

WHATEVER the mission of life may be,
Let love keep true and let thought keep free;
And never, whatever the cause of the plan,
Enlarge the calling to lessen the man.
The cut of a coat,
Cant chatter'd by rote,
A priestly or princely state remote,
Whatever cajole
Away from The Whole
Is a clog and a curse to The Infinite's soul.
For God who made us made only a man,
No arms of a snob, no shield of a clan.
Far better a friend that is friendly to God
Than a sycophant kissing a ribbon or rod.

However the habits of life be vying,
Naught bound by a bias is worth the trying;
No sport whence the home must weep and wait
The step of a wanderer tarrying late;
No scheme with a lie
For a party-cry

To catch the lowly or court the high;
No faith of a fold
Where love is enroll'd
For a test no bigger than badge of gold.
Pause ere you try it: wherever is right,
The truth is clearer, the longer the sight.
Pause not: you prove the thought I am on;
Your soul is a slave, and your manhood gone.

By the author of "Haydn."

LIFE BELOW;

IN SEVEN POEMS.

NOTICES OF THE PRESS.

Of parts of the book published separately: "Poems by an anonymous author, who writes vigorously, and proves that he is no novice in poetical composition. His lines are well balanced, and read harmoniously. There are some passages worth remembering in each poem; and throughout the whole there is much freedom of expression, and a reflective tone that will favorably impress the lover of sensible verses."—*London Public Opinion.*

"The singer is a man whose experience indicates a depth of nature, whose political and moral philosophy seem in the main healthy, whose mastery of picturesque speech is something really noticeable, whose verse has both fire and sweetness, and who now and then crams a great thought into a gem of an expression, and thus effects a sacred marriage between strength and beauty. He has the elements of a true poet."—*Dover Morning Star.*

"Unless we are mistaken, the book will attract no inconsiderable attention. We are particularly pleased with the first poem, entitled 'Choosing,' and regard it as marked by more than ordinary merit."—*American Literary Gazette and Public Circular.*

"These poems have merits such as we believe will not only disarm criticism but secure its favorable judgment." —*Christian Intelligencer.*

"They contain many glimpses of that subtle experience of the world which it is so difficult to photograph in words, and with some passages hazy and obscure contain many of great beauty. The anonymous author is a master of language and rhythm as well as much of a thinker." —*New York Evangelist.*

"The verse is musical and flowing, with a rich cadence and rhythmic swing. A delicate fancy plays over the plan of the poems, and interweaves itself into the separate yet united parts. The verses have much real merit." —*Louisville* (Ky.) *Democrat.*

"The production of a young poet of more than common promise." —*Princeton Review.*

"The poems are very far from being a simple narrative of an eventful life. The life is in fact only the string around which discussions on all points of morals and social life are crystallized. .... There are many good things in the book." —*Cincinnati Journal and Messenger.*

ANALYSIS OF LIFE BELOW.

THE seven poems of this book are supposed to be written in a country village in the northern part of the United States during the time of the recent civil war. An aged author and reformer, who has allowed his amanuensis to enter the army, dictates the different poems, which relate his own personal history, to different characters in the village who volunteer to assist him.

He chooses his assistants according to their ages, dictating the youngest part of his life to the youngest of them, and so on successively. Every scribe is supposed to be at the same period of life as was the reformer at the time of the experience which he is recalling. This arrangement affords an opportunity to sketch, in the person of each scribe, the results appearing to the eyes of the world of the traits of character whose hidden experience is related in the successive poems. Thus life is completely represented, both in its subjective and objective developments. The first of these sketches is contained in the passage entitled

DO.

Introduction: and the first and lowest outward report of the ascending stages of inner experience, the first of which is related in

POEM FIRST. — CHOOSING.

1. Circumstances summoning choice to exercise are often trifling, 2. beautiful, hence attractive. 3. Introduction to narrative of such a circumstance. 4. Sunset described. 5. It assumes the appearance of a city. 6–8. Reflection and desire for light suggested thereby. 9. Dream following reflection (which may apply to experience while discovering a special truth, or general truth, or wisdom sought through an entire life of a man or of the race); city opens and light approaches. 10. Digression: Power of Expression. 11, 12. Song heard amid the light. 13. Its source, a chariot with messenger. 14. Her invitation; the dreamer's acceptance. 15. Journey past bounds of time. 16. Her description. 17. The dreamer's experience; the realm of whims (the supernatural in detail, to which causes assigned are) 18. Fairies. 19. Fairy chariot. 20. Fairy song. 21. Dissipation of whims. 22. Reason assigned them. 23. Existence of the supernatural. 24. The realm of wisdom (the supernatural collectively); the temple. 25. Arrival there. 26. Entrance. 27.

Invitation of interior. 28. Enthusiasm in anticipation of light: The flight to 29. the dome (comprehensiveness of truth). 30. The altar (absoluteness of truth): the seven stages of "Life Below" prefigured. 31. The aisles radiating from the altar (complexity of truth). 32. The dreamer allowed to find out the truth in the aisles 33. of material aims. 34. Mental aims. 35. Emotional aims. 36. His failure to discover truth, and prayer at the altar. 37. The answer to faith. 38. Light imparted from its source, whereby truth is discovered in the aisles 39. and love at the altar. 40. Song of the world's redemption. 41. End of the dream; effect on the dreamer. 42. His faith stimulated to live true to self, in dreams and desires 43. in order thus to live true to others. 44. That all may do the same, the necessity of charity 45. for each in his own sphere that he may venture, perhaps fail, at least learn faith, 46. the end of Choosing.

RE.

Second outward report of inner life.

POEM SECOND. — DARING.

1. Night. 2. The hero. 3, 4. Flight from home. 5. Its occasion. 6. Slavery. 7. Emancipation. 8–10. The Farewell. 11–13. Digression: Upon growing old. 14. Resumption of narrative. 15. The farmer. 16, 17. His welcome. 18. The breakfast. 19, 20. The discussion thereat. 21–23. The farmer's railway-speech. 24, 25. His conclusion. 26, 27. The hero disheartened. 28. He revives. 29. The gossips. 30. Poetry of railway-riding. 31. The fellow-travellers. 32. The physician. 33. The banker's words. 34. The physician's answer. 35. The hero's answer. 36. Their insult. 37. His rejoinder. 38. Its effect. 39. Philosophy of childhood. 40. Despondency. 41–44. Home-sickness. 45. The new friend. 46. His request. 47. Is made a confidant. 48. Describes his guardian. 49. Bal-

timore. 50. Hope realized. 51. The boarding-school. 52. Its matron. 53. Its tutor. 54. Unartificial piety. 55. Its influence. 56–58. Boy-life. 59. Its reading. 60. Its rudeness. 61. Its rashness. 62. Its chastenings. 63. Immutability of love. 64–66. The hero criticised. 67–69. His answer to the critic, 70. to his tutor. 71. Egotism a misrepresentation. 72. The hero misjudged and sentenced. 73. Power of love (1) in imparting truth, proved either *(a)* from premises agreed upon; 74. hence necessity of sympathy; 75. or *(b)* from intuitions common to all; hence the same necessity. 76. (2) In imparting love, communicated either from love to man; 77, or love to God. 78. Examples. 79. Necessity of faith in love *per se.* 80. The tutor's application. 81. Effect on the hero. 82. Training of the world. 83. The hero's dream. 84. His awaking. 85. His second flight. 86. The storm. 87. Midnight in the streets. 88. The criminal. 89–91. Sunrise. 92. The slumberer. 93. Conclusion.

ME.

Third outward report of inner life.

POEM THIRD. — DOUBTING.

1. Solitary condition of the doubter. 2. Craves appreciation. 3. Fretted by disesteem. Anger. 4. Its influence. 5. Faith in self, the source of faith from others; conquest the road to crowning. 6. Home of the hero. 7. Its inmates. 8. Its pastimes. 9. Loneliness. 10. Morbidness. 11. Excuse of the recluse. 12. Midnight thoughts of suicide. 13. Insanity. 14. Personal responsibility — for exercise of will (in the), 15, use of opportunity (and), 16, use of inherent disposition (while), 17, developing, despite pesterings of prejudice, the mission of the individual (and doing one's), 18, duty to others. 19. Obstacles, from without, material means: 20. from within, mental weakness. 21. Yielding to circumstances. 22. Pleasure unmasked. 23.

Solace in society. 24. Faith, an element of friendship. 25. Social curiosity. 26. Hypocrisy. 27. Gossip. 28. Scandal. 29. Refuge in self—The lesson of loneliness. 30. Philosophy, its pleasures. 31. Its perils. 32. Its certainty. 33. Its uncertainty—The vanity of fame. 34. The Church. 35. Hymn. 36. Its effect. 37. The sermon; the sovereignty of truth, applied to individual desires and deeds, and to the elevation of the community. 38. Faith, 39. the object of experience. 40. The fruition of individuality.

FA.

Fourth outward report of inner life.

POEM FOURTH.—LEARNING.

1. Faith bewildered by teachings of men turns to thoughts of God in nature. 2. A grove by moonlight. 3. Brook in the grove. 4. Sounds in the grove. 5. Effect of, upon the spirit; the stranger (symbolical of the genius of nature, who discourses upon the THEOLOGY OF NATURE). 6. The supernatural. 7, 8. Feticism better than no faith. 9. Man dependent on material nature; 10. yet a personality. 11. His dependence causes sympathy between mind and matter, influencing mind by thoughts of God in matter. 12. His personality makes him priest of nature. 13. Thoughts of God in mind as well as matter. 14. Mind, with sin, retains His image and is guided by His Spirit (to be proved by an appeal to Theology, as manifested consecutively in human consciousness and in teachings of divine revelation). 15. The realm of history. 16. (Symbolical) journey to the place of view. 17. Mountain musings. 18. (THEOLOGY IN CONSCIOUSNESS). *1st historical view:* India, and the cosmology of the Hindoo: 19. of other nations; conceptions of one Creator; of the Trinity. 20. *2d historical view:* Chaldee; and rise of idolatry; conception of divine providence. 21. *3d historical view:* Persia; and the power of evil. 22. Conception of human sin, and the Tempter.

23. A storm described. 24. *4th historical view:* Greece, and holy mounts; heaven-sent laws; conception of results of sin; fear appeased by sacrifices. 25. Question: why reverence heathenism? Answer: Had some truth in spirit, though false in form. 26. (THEOLOGY IN REVELATION). *5th historical view:* Egypt, and traditions of Noah; death of Osiris. 27. His resurrection; expectations of a future Saviour; the atonement. 28. Question: What profit the Jew? Answer: The chosen priest-nation; yet to minister to humanity; how fitted for this. 29. How unfitted; through bigotry; neglect of revelation; of history; of consciousness; of spirituality. 30. A view confirmed by Biblical facts; and statements; and analogy of degeneration in Christendom. 31. *6th historical view:* Scandinavia, and destruction of the world. Under the Yggdrasill. 32. Description of; traditions of other trees. 33. Roots of the tree; home of the gods. 34. Their gathering for battle. 35. Their contest. 36. Destruction of the Universe. 37. Separation of good and evil. 38. Heaven. 39. *7th historical view:* Calvary delivering from sight of doom. 40. *8th historical view:* Christendom from Pentecost to present. 41. The Church. 42. The Israel of to-day; without the Temple has the Synagogue and its government. 43. Christian liberty; indicates Christ's sovereignty; as could not be done by a sovereignty of forms in deeds, 44. or in creeds; because true religion is of faith. 45. Christian liberty causes not anarchy; nor irreverence; nor indifference; but charity and spiritual unity. 46. *9th historical view:* The Church formal. 47. Its finiteness. 48. Result in ritualism, 49. in rationalism. 50. The Infinite Unity may cause finite differences; 51 does overrule them for good; 52. reveals all truth according to same analogy; 53. has revealed to all sufficient for salvation; though not for assurance, in order thus to stimulate search. 54. Duty of search; its ultimate success. 55. The farewell.

SOL.

Fifth outward report of inner life.

POEM FIFTH. — LOVING.

1. The conflict of life. 2. The law of the world; *i. e.*, separation. 3. Evinced in material nature; and in man, 4. in infancy. 5. The desire of the spirit; *i. e.*, 6, union, 7. counteracting the law of the world. 8. The infant on its mother's breast. 9. The mother. 10. Their separation. 11. The school. 12. Its sports. 13. Its cares. 14. Love looking away from home. 15. Friendships of childhood. 16. Romance. 17. The reverence of love. 18. The friend of youth. 19. Separations of youth. 20. The choice of a life-work. 21. The solitude of duty. 22. Truth to self. 23. The recompense of bigotry. 24. The reward of charity. 25. The recurrence of love. 26. Falling in love. 27. The transfigurations of love. 28. Disappointment in love. 29. The poetical *vs.* the practical. 30. A crime in common. 31. Jilted. 32. Struggle against love. 33. Death of the ideal. 34. Prostitution of enthusiasm. 35. Slavery to form. 36. Will and conversion. 37. Triumph of duty. 38. Reappearance of love. 39. Love awakened. 40. Broken friendship renewed. 41. Forgiveness. 42. The wife. 43. Self-depreciation of love. 44. Self-sufficiency of love. 45. Fear of a false ideal. 46. Deceitfulness of appearances. 47. Feeling and fidelity. 48. Separation risked through infidelity to social relations. 49. Through analogous infidelity to God; The Fall of man. 50. Possibility of separation from God through self-confidence, the ground of union to Him through faith: the reason of The Fall. 51. Possibility of separation, the ground everywhere of spiritual unity — even in the Godhead. 52. Faith the reconciler of the law of the world, *i. e.* separation, and of the desire of the Spirit, *i. e.* union. 53. The Spirit, through faith, triumphant. Conclusion.

LA.

Sixth outward report of inner life.

POEM SIXTH. — SERVING.

1–4. The joys of home. 5. The immortality of love. 6. The hero of the poem. 7. His character. 8. His bearing. 9. His fidelity. 10. His reputation. 11. The misinterpretations of sincerity. 12. Of breadth. 13. Of intensity. 14. Of imagination. 15. Sensitiveness. 16. Affinity. 17, 18. Marriage. 19. Sickness. 20. Leaving home. 21. At Sea. 22–26. Apostrophe to the ocean. 27–30. Ireland. 31–33. Scotland. 34. The Yarrow. 35. Cumberland. 36. England. 37. The English home. 38. The Anglo-Saxon race. 39. Belgium. 40. Holland. 41. Church music. 42. Germany. 43. The Sabbath considered in itself; 44. in its relation to difference in race. 45. America caricatured. 46. Sabbath in relation to difference in government. 47. Religious training necessary in a republic. 48. Freedom of the German genius. 49. Its need of faith. 50. The revival in Italy. 51. The right of revolution. 52. The wrong of formalism. 53. Russia. 54. France, her moulding power. 55. Her imitators. 56. Her life and its deficiency. 57. The traveller. 58, 59. Apostrophe to America. 60. Resumption of the narrative. 61. Sad news from home. 62. The return voyage. 63. The arrival. 64. The Hudson. 65. The buried children. 66. Prayer, the outlet of sorrow. 67, 68. Tale of the wife. 69, 70. The hero's search for her. 71. The South. 72. The prairie. 73. The mountain home. 74, 75. The salvation of effort. 76. The universality of love. 77. The mistakes of misanthropy. 78–81. Sympathy. 82. Simplicity of truth. 83. Heaven an earth perfected. 84. Love the end of wisdom. 85. Infinity the goal of love. 86. Contentment. 87. The wanderer. 88, 89. The lost found. 90, 91. The rebuff. 92. The discipline of suffering. 93, 94. Perseverance. 95. The meeting. 96. Her excuse. 97. His answer. 98. Love reviving. 99, 102. The mission of love. 103. The reunion. 104. The second loss. 105, 106. The Farewell. 107–109. Conclusion.

SI.

Seventh outward report of inner life.

POEM SEVENTH. — WATCHING.

1. Life a unity through all experiences; to all persons; amid all circumstances; in all phases of existence. 2. Advantage of regarding life in more than one phase. 3. (1) Enthralls from confidence in (*a*) material laws. 4. (*b*) external appearances. 5. (*c*) human agency. 6. (2) It causes trust (*a*) in the spiritual power of truth; and (*b*) overruling of Providence. 7. Reference to a recent triumph of freedom evincing this. 8. Transition to subject of strife for freedom; (1) argument from Scripture. 9. Scripture principles apply equally to earth and heaven. 10. (2) Argument from reason in the form of visions. 11. Liberty as limited (*a*) by external conditions, found not (1) through separating from wills opposing; 12. nor (2) through uniting with wills agreeing; 13. nor (3) through submitting collectively to one human will governing; 14. because the source of slavery is internal. 15. Liberty as limited (*b*) by internal conditions, found (1) through knowledge of God. 16. (2) Through desire to do his will. 17. Effect of law in causing knowledge of God. 18. Effect of love in causing desire to do His will. 19. God the Alpha and Omega; source of love to inspire and truth to allure, 20. for both the race and the individual. 21. Analogy between a man and mankind. 22. The secret of individual success. 23. National progress. 24. The coming day, its love. 25. Its light. 26. Its liberty. 27. Tyranny of established forms. 28. Freedom from established

forms, where? 29. Tribute to America. 30. Transition. 31. Apostrophe to youth, as the embodiment of the new; 32. as the confidence of hope, 33. awaiting success upon earth, 34. awaiting immortality. 35. The belief in immortality of the soul 36. is universal, 37. necessary to interpret life. 38. Doubts concerning it. 39. Confuted by reference to (*a*) constant growth of the soul. 40. (*b*) Its essence. 41. (*c*) Its powers. 42. (*d*) Its performances. 43. (*e*). The character of Him who gives it faith. 44. The reward of faith. 45. A prayer for progress. 46. Conclusion.

DO.

Eighth outward report of inner life; the last note in the ascending scale of life below, the first in the scale of life above.

www.ingramcontent.com/pod-product-compliance
Lightning Source LLC
LaVergne TN
LVHW011234110826
845150LV00006B/1635

* 9 7 8 1 4 2 5 5 1 4 5 3 2 *